The "Thumbs-Up" Man

The "Thumbs-Up" Man

... And 30 Other Bible-Based Meditations

Roger Ellsworth and his family

Unless otherwise noted, Scripture quotations are taken from the New King James Version®. Copyright © 1982 by Thomas Nelson. Used by permission. All rights reserved..

Copyright © 2017, Roger Ellsworth

All rights reserved. No part of this book may be reproduced, scanned, or distributed in any printed or electronic form without permission.

First Edition: 2017

ISBN: 978-0-9988812-5-6

20170807LSI

Great Writing Publications
www.greatwriting.org
Taylors, SC

www.greatwriting.org

Purpose

My Coffee Cup Meditations are short, easy-to-read, engagingly presented devotions based on the Bible, the Word of God. Each reading takes a single idea or theme and develops it in a thought-provoking way so that you are inspired to consider the greatness of God, the relevance of the good news of the life, death, resurrection, and coming-again of Jesus, and are better equipped for life in this world and well prepared for the world to come.

www.mycoffeecupmeditations.com

https://www.facebook.com/MyCoffeeCupMeditations/

Dedication

Dedicated to the dear saints at
First Baptist Church, Greenfield, Tennessee

About This Book

This book is a combined effort, the result of the labors of the family of Roger and Sylvia Ellsworth. You may read more about them on page 141.

Each reading reflects the character of its author, so you will be able to enjoy a range of writing styles and tastes.

Under the title of each chapter, there is a note to tell you who the writer is.

We hope you will enjoy these Bible-based meditations. We would love to hear from you, so please send us a note to tell us what you think—which ones you liked most, and how they made a difference in your life or in the life of a family member, friend, or work associate. To reach us online, go to www.mycoffeecupmeditations.com/contact

MEDITATIONS

Table of Contents

1 The "Thumbs-Up" Man 16
2 That Terrible, Terrific Moment 20
3 Our Gulf-Spanning God 24
4 Saying Goodbye to a World of Goodbyes 28
5 Thanks for the Thoughts 32
6 Even My Cap Knows I've Been Saved! 36
7 God Leads His Dear Children 40
8 The Way of the Righteous 44
9 How Will We Be Remembered? 48
10 The Fretful Clock 52
11 Unsung Heroes 56
12 Wisdom for the Life Business 60
13 Words to the Bride 64
14 The Therapy of Thanks in the Thick of Things 68
15 I Want to Hear Bert Wilson Pray Again 72
16 Hard Thoughts about God 76
17 My Sanctified Dog, Gus 80
18 Our Need-Meeting God 84
19 Who Like Me? 88
20 Dad's Old Bible 92
21 Getting the Hallelujah Back (1) 96
22 Getting the Hallelujah Back (2) 100
23 Seeing from Heaven's Glory with Heaven's Eyes 104
24 The New Dress 108
25 The Wonderful Cross 112

26 God's Prescription for an Age-Old Malady	116
27 The Ups and Downs of Faith	120
28 Lord, Help Me to Spaffordize	124
29 Can You Bear to Let Them Go?	128
30 A Death That Led to Life	132
31 A Throne Set in Heaven	136
About the Authors	141

The App

www.mycoffeecupmeditations.com

Be sure you get the app!

-1-

From God's Word, the Bible...

But I do not want you to be ignorant, brethren, concerning those who have fallen asleep, lest you sorrow as others who have no hope. For if we believe that Jesus died and rose again, even so God will bring with Him those who sleep in Jesus.

For this we say to you by the word of the Lord, that we who are alive and remain until the coming of the Lord will by no means precede those who are asleep. For the Lord Himself will descend from heaven with a shout, with the voice of an archangel, and with the trumpet of God. And the dead in Christ will rise first. Then we who are alive and remain shall be caught up together with them in the clouds to meet the Lord in the air. And thus we shall always be with the Lord. Therefore comfort one another with these words.

1 Thessalonians 4:13-18

The "Thumbs-Up" Man

(A Reading from Roger)

It was a long time ago, but it is still firmly etched in my mind. What's that? The image of meeting Lester Auten very early each weekday morning! He would be driving to his work in his old pickup truck and I would be driving to my study. I used to tease him about that truck. It had so many holes in it that I dubbed it a "see-through" truck.

The thing I most remember about those Monday-through-Friday meetings is not the sight of his beat-up pickup. It is rather what Pete—that's what we called him—would do when he spotted me. He would smile and give me the thumbs-up sign. I never asked him about it. I never felt like I needed an explanation. I took his thumbs-up sign to mean: "Be encouraged! Everything is going to be okay!"

I know God is in control and that He makes no mistakes, but in my little, limited perspective, Pete left us much too soon. He died at age fifty-six on March 1, 1996. It was a crushing loss.

Pete was a good and godly man. He was a churchman.

He loved his church and was very concerned to protect her from apathy, heresy, and division. He had little patience with those who spoke ill of her or of her pastor.

Pete had no say over the date of his birth or the date of his death. But he sure had a lot to say about that dash between the two, and he said it very well.

I'm sure Pete had his critics and detractors, but I never heard anyone speak disparagingly of him. The men of his Bible class thought so highly of him that they re-named their class after his death. What did they call it? The Thumbs-Up Class!

Ask me today about Pete Auten, and I will say "Faithful friend and a joy forever."

It was the gospel of Christ that made Pete the man he was. He loved the gospel. In his younger years, he came to see the reality and the depth of his sins and that he was not in himself prepared to stand in the presence of the holy God. He also came to see that the Lord Jesus went to the cross of Calvary to receive the wrath of God in the place of sinners. Because Jesus received it, no wrath remains for all who repent of their sins and trust in Him and the work He did on that cross. Pete could joyfully sing John Newton's words:

> *Amazing grace! How sweet the sound,*
> *That saved a wretch like me!*
> *I once was lost, but now am found,*
> *Was blind, but now I see.*

> *'Twas grace that taught my heart to fear,*
> *And grace my fears relieved;*
> *How precious did that grace appear*
> *The hour I first believed!*

It fell to me to preach at Pete's funeral. I've had to do lots of hard things in my years as a pastor, but that, I think, has to rank as the hardest of them all. In the sermon, I made mention of meeting Pete each weekday and of him smiling and giving me the thumbs-up sign. In my closing words, I expressed my firm conviction that I will, because of the glorious grace of Christ, see Pete again. I fully expect when I encounter him in the air (1 Thess. 4:17) to see him flash that familiar thumbs-up sign once again. And there everything will finally be okay. I will not be there because of anything good I have done, and he will not be there because of anything good he did. We will both be there because of the good Jesus did for us by His perfect life and atoning death.

-2-

From God's Word, the Bible...

Now we know that whatever the law says, it says to those who are under the law, that every mouth may be stopped, and all the world may become guilty before God. Therefore by the deeds of the law no flesh will be justified in His sight, for by the law is the knowledge of sin.

Romans 3:19-20

The Terrible, Terrific Moment

(A Reading from Roger)

As a teenager, William R. Newell was so rebellious that he brought continual heartache to his parents. His father, a pastor, pleaded with R.A. Torrey, President of Moody Bible College, to accept his son as a student. Torrey refused. The father continued to plead, and Torrey finally agreed.

While he was at Moody, Newell encountered the Word of God in a new and powerful way and became a Christian. What did God's Word do for him? He gives us the answer in his well-known hymn *At Calvary*:

> *By God's Word at last my sin I learned*
> *Then I trembled at the law I'd spurned.*

It was for Newell both a terrible and terrific moment. Terrible? Absolutely! It is a terrible thing to learn the truth about ourselves. And the truth is that we are all sinners, and sin is an awesomely horrible thing. What is sin? It is refusing to conform to what God requires. It is refusing to live according to God's laws. It is thumbing our noses in the face of our Creator and saying, "We will not live they way You want us to live. We will live the way we want to live."

God is not only our Creator. He is also our Judge. We must all give account of ourselves to Him (Rom. 14:12; Heb. 9:27). If we stand before Him in our sins, He will most surely drive us from His presence.

For several years Newell had lived without regard to his sins or to the God that he was destined to meet. He had lived in "vanity and pride." But in that terrible moment when he was confronted by God's Word, he "trembled" at the law, God's law, that he had "spurned." To spurn something is to reject it with an attitude of contempt or disdain.

Imagine it! Going through life without knowing anything about God's laws or knowing about them and not caring! Then it hits you one day that this God is real, that you have to meet Him, and all your life you have been a "spurner." You go through the Ten Commandments, and you realize that you have broken each one again and again. You are a law-breaker who must stand before the law-giver. It's no wonder that Newell said he "trembled at the law" he had "spurned." How could he, a law-breaker, ever stand acceptably in the presence of the holy law-giver?

But Newell's terrible moment was also his terrific moment. When people realize that they are sinners and begin to tremble over their sins and the judgment to come, they are in a position to receive God's remedy for law-breakers. That remedy? It is Calvary, the place where the Lord Jesus Christ was crucified.

By the grace of God, Newell came to understand that Jesus was not on that cross to pay for His own law-breaking because He, Jesus, never broke any of God's laws (1 John

3:5). He was there to receive the penalty for our law-breaking—eternal separation from God—so all who received Him would never have to pay that same penalty. What an astounding thing! On the cross, the law-giver took the penalty of law-breakers! And because Jesus took it, there is now no penalty for those who do as Newell did and turn to Christ.

In his hymn, Newell looks back over his life and expresses double amazement. He is amazed at how he had lived and amazed that there could be pardon for one who had lived as he had. Try to imagine the joy he felt when he penned these lines:

> *Mercy there was great, and grace was free;*
> *Pardon there was multiplied to me;*
> *There my burdened soul found liberty,*
> *At Calvary.*

In John Bunyan's *The Pilgrim's Progress*, the major character, Christian, came to the cross, gave three leaps for joy, and went on singing…

> *Thus far did I come laden with my sin,*
> *Nor could aught ease the grief that I was in,*
> *Till I came hither. What a place is this!*
> *Must here be the beginning of my bliss!*

The greatest of all knowledge is to know ourselves to be sinners. It will be terrible when we come to know that, but that knowledge will lead us on to that which is terrific indeed—salvation through Christ.

-3-

From God's Word, the Bible...

For there is one God and one Mediator between God and men, the Man Christ Jesus, who gave Himself a ransom for all, to be testified in due time...

1 Timothy 2:5-6

Our Gulf-Spanning God

(A Reading from Sylvia)

The great hymns of the church are a wonderful part of our Christian heritage. They teach great biblical truths and express our praise to God for those truths. Many hymns have nuggets of gold in the space of just a few words. The hymn *At Calvary*, written by William R. Newell, has these words at the end of verse 4:

> *Oh, the mighty gulf that God did span*
> *At Calvary.*

Have you ever given much thought to the mighty gulf that God spanned at Calvary? The more you understand about that mighty gulf, the more precious your salvation will become to you. What is that mighty gulf? It is the vast expanse between a holy God and sinful man. It is an expanse so very wide that no man can bridge it on his own. In fact no one, no matter how good he perceives himself to be, can even come close to bridging that gap.

We know that God is holy, but it isn't easy for us to comprehend exactly what that means. God is perfect in every aspect of His being. He is perfectly perfect. We also know that we are sinners. But that, too, is difficult for us to completely comprehend. Just as every aspect of God's being is perfect, so every aspect of our being is tainted with sin. Our sinful actions, our sinful words, our sinful thoughts are ever present in our lives as sins of commission. And then there are the sins of omission—the good actions we fail to do, the kind, positive words we fail to speak, and the godly thoughts we fail to entertain.

There is indeed a mighty gulf between sinful man and holy God that we cannot possibly span. But if we are ever to be acceptable to God and to have any hope of God letting us into heaven (Rev. 21:27), that gulf must somehow be spanned. God cannot un-god himself and come down to our level, and we cannot make ourselves perfect, no matter how hard we try.

So God in His great wisdom devised a plan to span that gap. His Son, Jesus Christ, became the God-man by taking our humanity without divesting himself of His deity. He lived the perfect life required of us that we cannot possibly live. He went to Calvary's cross and became sin for us and there received the wrath of God against that sin in our place (2 Cor. 5:21). A marvelous exchange takes place for believers. Jesus took our sin and we get His righteousness. God accepted what Jesus did as evidenced by the resurrection. Thus Jesus Christ became the bridge that spanned that great gulf between sinful man and holy God.

And why did God go to such great length to do this? The hymn writer gives us the answer in the first lines of this same verse:

Oh, the love that drew salvation's plan!
Oh, the grace that brought it down to man!

It was God's great love for us and His grace to us that moved His heart to devise salvation's plan and bring it down to man. In our limited knowledge, we cannot fully comprehend that kind of love and grace. In eternity I believe that God will reveal to us layer after layer of His great love and grace, and we will forever praise Him for salvation's plan. What a God of wisdom, love, and grace we serve! Oh, the mighty gulf that God did span at Calvary. All praise and glory to our great gulf-spanning God.

-4-

From God's Word, the Bible...

These all died in faith, not having received the promises, but having seen them afar off were assured of them embraced them and confessed that they were strangers and pilgrims on the earth. For those who say such things declare plainly that they seek a homeland. And truly if they had called to mind that country from which they had come out, they would have had opportunity to return. But now they desire a better, that is, a heavenly country. Therefore God is not ashamed to be called their God, for He has prepared a city for them.

Hebrews 11:13-16

Saying Goodbye to a World of Goodbyes

(A Reading from Roger)

I have often had to say "Goodbye." Many times it has been a pleasure. When I completed my years of education, it was a joy to say goodbye to boring lectures, tons of homework, and tests. I shall never forget saying goodbye to the hospital where I had surgery to repair a skull fracture. That was a wonderful goodbye indeed.

But the majority of my goodbyes have been painful. A few years back, I had to say goodbye to my father, and a few years after that to my mother. There have been goodbyes to churches I have served as pastor. Those have always been difficult. And there have been goodbyes to dear friends.

Dog-lovers will understand this (and if you're not one, please go to the next paragraph)—it is exceedingly hard to say goodbye to a true and loyal canine friend.

I realize that I have had to say fewer goodbyes than some, and many of my goodbyes have not been as difficult as those experienced by others. I try to keep these things in mind so I can keep my balance and not turn my life into an ongoing pity party. But I have had my share, and I am sure you have as well. This is a world of goodbyes.

My sad goodbyes here make me look forward to that time in which I will be able to say a final goodbye—a goodbye to this world of goodbyes!

Yes, I am looking forward to that world in which there will be no more goodbyes. I'm talking about that world the Bible calls heaven.

Heaven consists of two stages or states. There is the intermediate state and the final state. The intermediate state is the one which the soul enters when the believer dies. His or her body goes into the grave, and the soul goes to be with God. But that is not the final state. The Lord Jesus is going to come again, bringing as He comes the souls of all believers who have died. He is going to raise the bodies of believers and those bodies, modeled after His own resurrection body, will be rejoined to those souls. In those resurrected, glorified bodies, believers will inhabit what is described in Revelation 21 and 22, that is, a new earth which will have one glorious city—the New Jerusalem (Rev. 21:2).

One feature of that new world puzzled me for a long time. The Apostle John says: " ... there was no more sea" (Rev. 21:1). I wondered about that. Why will there be no sea on that new earth? Then it occurred to me that the sea has often been the place of separation or the place of sad goodbyes. One loved one is on the ship while another stands on the shore, and they wave goodbye. There will be no such separation in heaven and no need to say goodbye. This is the destiny of all who have repented of their sins and trusted in the Lord Jesus Christ as their Savior.

While I wait for my new body and my new world, and while I continue to say sad goodbyes here, I try to sing along with Squire Parsons:

> *I'm kind of homesick for a country*
> *To which I've never been before.*
> *No sad goodbyes will there be spoken*
> *For time won't matter anymore.*
>
> *Beulah Land, I'm longing for you*
> *And some day on thee I'll stand.*
> *There my home shall be eternal.*
> *Beulah Land, sweet Beulah Land.*
>
> *I'm looking now across the river*
> *Where my faith will end in sight.*
> *There's just a few more days to labor.*
> *Then I will take my heavenly flight.*[1]

---

[1] "Sweet Beulah Land Lyrics." *Lyrics.com*. STANDS4 LLC, 2017. Web. 6 Jul 2017. <http://www.lyrics.com/lyric/5214769>.

-5-

From God's Word, the Bible...

Many, O LORD my God, are Your wonderful works
Which You have done;
And Your thoughts toward us
Cannot be recounted to You in order;
If I would declare and speak of them,
They are more than can be numbered.

Psalm 40:5

Thanks for the Thoughts

(A Reading from Roger)

How often does it occur to us to give thanks to God for His thoughts toward us? We often express thanks to various ones for their thoughtfulness. Do we realize as we should that no one has been more thoughtful toward us than God?

In Psalm 40 David gives thanks to God. He begins with the particular and moves to the general. He thinks about a harrowing crisis from which God had delivered him (vv. 1-2) and that causes him to think about some general things. He thanks God for His "wonderful works" which are "many," and then he mentions the thoughts of God.

It is as if David is saying something along these lines: "This wonderful deliverance that I have experienced is just one of God's many wonderful works, and all His wonderful works flow from Him thinking about me."

So let's think about the thoughts of God and let's thank Him for the thoughts.

It occurs to me that it is a staggering thing that God would think about us at all. The chasm between God and us is too huge for words. He is almighty in strength, unlimited in wisdom, and clothed in majesty and glory. We are weak, foolish, and wear the tattered garments of sin. Yet God thinks about us! No wonder David marveled:

> *What is man that You are mindful of him?*
> (Ps. 8:4)

Then it is amazing that God has as many thoughts about us as He does. It would be a wonderful thing indeed if God had only a thought or two toward us, but His thoughts about us are "more than can be numbered" (v. 3).

David says God's thoughts "cannot be recounted … in order." If we were to attempt to relate all the thoughts God has had toward us in the order in which He had them, we would be attempting the impossible. It would be as impossible as moving Mt. Everest with a spoon. In Psalm 139:17-18, David says:

> *How precious also are Your thoughts to me, O God!*
> *If I should count them, they would be more in number than the sand…*

It is further amazing that God would think about us the thoughts that He thinks. Someone might be inclined to say, "I'm sure God thinks about me. He thinks about making my life miserable."

The devil would have you believe that, but he is the master of lies, and that is one of his lies. Here is what God says about His thoughts toward His people: "For I know the thoughts that I think toward you, says the LORD, thoughts of peace and not of evil, to give you a future and a hope" (Jer. 29:11).

To all of that we must add this: It is astonishing that God would think about us in the greatest way possible. And what way is that? It is God thinking about the way to forgive us of our sins and to restore us to Himself. And God found the way. That way is none other than His Son, Jesus Christ.

This fortieth Psalm is Messianic. That means it looks forward to the coming of the Lord Jesus Christ. I can hear Him say to the Father the words of verses 7 and 8:

> *Behold, I come;*
> *In the scroll of the Book it is written of me.*
> *I delight to Your will, O my God,*
> *And Your law is within my heart.*

Jesus came to this earth in our humanity just as He and the Father had agreed. He came to do the will of the Father, that is, He came to perfectly obey the laws of God, which, of course, we have not obeyed. And His obedience was not grudging but flowed from a heart that loved the law of God.

One thing the law of God demands is payment for sin. Through His life, the Lord Jesus provided the righteousness we lack, and through His death He received the penalty for our sins.

All of this is because God thought toward us the greatest thought of all! How thankful we should be for all His thoughts and for this one thought in particular!

-6-

From God's Word, the Bible...

Therefore, if anyone is in Christ, he is a new creation; old things have passed away; behold, all things have become new.

2 Corinthians 5:17

Even My Cap Knows I've Been Saved!

(A Reading from Roger)

The words came from Burliss Hill in a Baptist testimony meeting a couple of weeks after his conversion to Christ. More about that cap in a minute!

Before he was converted, Burliss was a rough, hot-tempered man. It was my father who invited him to attend revival services at a nearby Baptist church. Burliss agreed to go. When the service was over, he angrily stomped away telling my Dad not to invite him again because he wouldn't be back. Much to my Dad's surprise, he was back the next night and for several nights in succession. Each time he went away angry and swore that he would not return. But there was an invisible hand at work drawing Burliss in.

One night my parents were awakened by someone rapping on their door. They opened the door and there stood Burliss' wife, Hilda, saying: "You've got to come, Burliss is trying to find the Lord."

My parents went. My Dad prayed with Burliss, and he was, to use a phrase that was common in those days, gloriously saved.

Now about that cap! Before he was saved, Burliss was given to great outbursts of temper. In his fits of rage he would invariably throw his cap on the ground and stomp on it. But his conversion to Christ made him a new man. Burliss knew that he was new, and, in his estimation, his cap knew as well because he had not stomped on it since he was saved!

Burliss Hill would answer God's call to preach the gospel and would become my parents' pastor and my pastor. He preached the morning that I was converted, and he baptized me in the pond of a local farmer a few days later.

Burliss was a common, ordinary man who loved the Lord and faithfully preached His Word. I will always be grateful to God for him.

I'm sure most consider me to be hopelessly out of date and old-fashioned, but I believe in those things so wonderfully portrayed in the conversion of Burliss Hill. I believe that there is such a thing as conviction of sin and that it can be so powerful that it drives sinners to despair. I believe that there is salvation in Christ for even the worst of sinners. I believe that salvation changes people, that if anyone is truly saved he is, in the words of Paul, "a new creation" and that "old things have passed away" and "all things have become new" (2 Cor. 5:17).

I often wonder these days what has happened to those days. Where are those who are under a heavy conviction from the Spirit of God? An old hymn, *Brethren, We Have Met to Worship*, refers to "trembling mourners, who are struggling hard with sin." That line must sound very strange to the few people who still sing that hymn!

Where are those who are "gloriously saved"? And why is

it that so many who profess faith in Christ give no evidence of a profound change and soon fall away?

And where are the pastors who preach for a deep conviction of sin and a glorious salvation? Much preaching these days seems more interested in amusing sinners than in convicting them and pointing them to Christ. In his hymn *At Calvary*, William R. Newell says:

> *By God's Word at last my sin I learned;*
> *Then I trembled at the law I'd spurned,*
> *Till my guilty soul imploring turned*
> *To Calvary.*

It is accurate and Spirit-anointed preaching of the Word of God that makes sinners learn about their sins, to tremble at the law they have spurned, and then to turn to Calvary. But what if the Word of God is not preached as it should be? Yes, what then?

These things must ultimately come, of course, from the Spirit of God, and that leads to another question: Where are those who are crying out for an unusual and powerful outpouring of God's Spirit?

If we are not now among those crying to God, let's make it our business to be among them. And let's believe that our crying will lead the Lord to say: "And I will not hide My face from them anymore; for I shall have poured out My Spirit…" (Ezek. 39:29).

-7-

From God's Word, the Bible...

But now, thus says the LORD, who created you, O Jacob,
And He who formed you, O Israel:
"Fear not, for I have redeemed you;
I have called you by your name;
You are Mine.
When you pass through the waters, I will be with you;
And through the rivers, they shall not overflow you.
When you walk through the fire, you shall not be burned,
Nor shall the flame scorch you."

Isaiah 43:1-2

God Leads His Dear Children

(A Reading from Sylvia)

When I recently heard a recording of the old hymn, *God Leads Us Along*, it brought back fond memories of my childhood and teen years at Steel City Baptist Church outside Benton, Ilinois. I thought of dear Hazel Bethel Wayman singing that hymn during many church services. The hymn was written by George A. Young in 1903. Young himself was no stranger to difficulty and hardship. For many years he served as a pastor of small churches in small communities, often finding it very difficult to make ends meet financially.

That brings me back to Hazel Bethel Wayman, who was just Hazel Bethel when I first became acquainted with her. She was a single mother whose husband had left her penniless with four children and one soon to be born. She and her children lived in a tiny, run-down house. They had no automobile and were very poor even by 1950s standards. Hazel Bethel's life was extremely difficult and yet this quiet, godly lady would stand in front of our small congregation and sing without accompaniment:

> *Some thro' the waters, some through the flood,*
> *Some thro' the fire, but all thro' the blood.*
> *Some thro' great sorrow, but God gives a song*
> *In the night season and all the day long.*

Even as a child I realized that God had certainly taken this dear lady through many hardships, described as water, flood, and fire by this hymn writer. But God had also taken her through the blood of Jesus Christ and given her a song in spite of her difficult life.

The second verse has these words:

> *Sometimes in the valley, in darkest of night,*
> *God leads His dear children along.*

I knew Hazel Bethel had gone through many valleys of darkest night. I wondered how many sleepless nights she had spent weeping and praying for God to take care of her and her children. God answered that prayer, and all five of her children grew to be responsible adults and committed Christians.

Verse three says:

> *Though sorrows befall us and Satan oppose,*
> *God leads His dear children along.*
> *Through grace we can conquer,*
> *Defeat all our foes;*
> *God leads His dear children along.*

By God's grace Hazel Bethel was a conqueror, defeating her foes of desertion and poverty. Her victory over being deserted by her husband was defeated by her knowledge that God had not deserted her. Her victory over poverty was not due to her becoming financially wealthy, but rather by her knowledge of the riches she possessed in Christ Jesus as her Savior and sustainer.

After her children were grown, Hazel Bethel became Hazel Wayman when God gave her a Christian husband. They enjoyed several years together before God took him home.

The last verse of this hymn has these lines:

> *Away from the mire, and away from the clay*
> *God leads His dear children along;*
> *Away up in glory, eternity's day,*
> *God leads His dear children along.*

Hazel Bethel Wayman was a living testimony to the Lord's sufficiency. She prevailed by God's grace, and she is now in the presence of her Lord and Savior, Jesus Christ, far removed from the mire and clay of this world. All her sorrows and dark nights are gone forevermore. I thank God for her life and for the godly example she was to one young girl. I remember her every time I hear that great hymn, *God Leads Us Along*.

-8-

From God's Word, the Bible...

Blessed is the man
Who walks not in the counsel of the ungodly,
Nor stands in the path of sinners, Nor sits in the seat of the scornful;
But his delight is in the law of the LORD,
And in His law he meditates day and night.
He shall be like a tree planted by the rivers of water,
That brings forth its fruit in its season,
Whose leaf also shall not wither; And whatever he does shall prosper.
The ungodly are not so,
But are like the chaff which the wind drives away.
Therefore the ungodly shall not stand in the judgment,
Nor sinners in the congregation of the righteous.
For the LORD knows the way of the righteous,
But the way of the ungodly shall perish.
Psalm 1

The Way of the Righteous

(A Reading from Martyn)

One of the most basic and fundamental truths of the Bible is that there are only two groups of people in the world. There are only two roads that people can travel. There are only two destinations to arrive at (Matt. 7:13-14).

Psalm 1 sets this division of the human race before us. It contrasts the righteous man and the ungodly man, the way of the righteous and the way of the wicked. In verses 1 to 3 the focus is on the walk or conduct of the righteous man. These verses emphasize four characteristics of the righteous man's life.

One is that it is *a blessed life* (v. 1). We often hear that when the Bible uses the word "blessed" it is using it as a synonym for "happy." It is true that the words are very similar, but the word "blessed" is a richer, fuller word. It speaks of God's favor resting upon someone, and of the joy, contentment, and fulfillment that person knows as a result of

God's favor. To be blessed is to know joy in God that does not depend upon circumstances. The Bible invariably joins these things together: righteousness and blessedness, holiness and happiness, walking in the fear of the Lord and experiencing true joy and contentment.

Another characteristic of the life of the righteous is that it is *a separated life*. Verse 1 describes the righteous man's life in terms of what it is not. The godly man does not walk in the counsel of the ungodly. In other words, he rejects the godless mindset of society. His life is not governed by the popular thinking or the accepted practices or the general consensus of the day. The righteous man also does not stand in the path of sinners. Standing indicates deliberate action. The man who does this is not merely coming under the influence of godless people as he goes along his way, but he is deliberately choosing the way of sinners. By contrast the righteous man does not linger in the path of sinners. Verse 1 also tells us that the righteous man does not sit in the seat of the scornful. This is a reference to the scoffer, the man who mocks God and ridicules all that is good and right and true. The way of the righteous is a separate way. The godly man separates himself from the counsel of the ungodly, the path of sinners, and the seat of the scornful.

A third mark of the righteous man's life is that it is *a Word-saturated life* (v. 2). The godly man delights in the law of the Lord. God's Word is a delight to the righteous man, and he demonstrates his delight by meditating upon it. We all think about what we love. If the Word of God is our delight, then we will spend much time reflecting upon it, pondering it, contemplating it. The truly blessed life is a life that is saturated with the Word of God.

A *fourth characteristic* of the righteous man's life is that it is *a flourishing life*. The man who saturates his life with God's Word will flourish like the tree described in verse 3. His life will be a beautiful thing. His life will be fruitful. His life will bring glory to God and be a source of blessedness to others.

Here are four questions to pose to yourself as you meditate upon Psalm 1.

- Are these verses an accurate description of your life?
- If not, why not?
- Do you want your life to be like this?
- What changes will you make?

Every child of God is, by definition, righteous. This term in the Old Testament applies to justified sinners and not to some elite class of Christians. However, God's people frequently backslide and live at a level in which they could hardly be said to be flourishing.

The good news is that if you are currently more like a shrub in the desert than like this well-watered tree in Psalm 1, there is grace with God to renew you, refresh you, and impart health to your soul. By God's grace you can become like this flourishing tree and know more of the blessedness spoken of in this Psalm.

-9-

From God's Word, the Bible...

He who troubles his own house will inherit the wind,
And the fool will be servant to the wise of heart.

Proverbs 11:29

How Will We Be Remembered?

(A Reading from Tim)

Some time ago an unusual obituary ran in a California newspaper. It was an obituary for a seventy-nine-year-old woman. It said: "Dolores had no hobbies, made no contribution to society, and rarely shared a kind word or deed in her life."

Her daughter, the writer of the obituary, also wrote: "I speak for the majority of her family when I say her presence will not be missed by many, very few tears will be shed, and there will be no lamenting over her passing."

What a way to be remembered!

A columnist from another newspaper investigated to determine if the obituary was legitimate or a hoax. Sadly, he verified its authenticity and even spoke to the daughter about what she had written. The woman explained: "I wanted to do the right thing, the honest thing. When she died, a co-worker gave me a copy of an obituary she wrote for her father as a kind of writing guide. What struck me was how my mother was none of the things I was reading. She was never there for us, she was never good, and she left no legacy."

It calls to mind what the Bible says when the vile, idolatrous king of Judah, Jehoram, died: "He reigned in Jerusalem eight years and, to no one's sorrow, departed" (2 Chron. 21:20).

What a contrast we have in the death of the godly priest Jehoiada: "But Jehoiada grew old and was full of days, and he died; he was one hundred and thirty years old when he died. And they buried him in the City of David among the kings, because he had done good in Israel, both toward God and His house" (2 Chron. 24:15-16).

The other day I picked up a copy of the book *A Nickel's Worth of Skim Milk*, written by Bob Hastings, a Baptist minister and editor for several years of *The Illinois Baptist*. The book is his story of growing up in southern Illinois.

My childhood experiences differ considerably from his. He was a child of the Great Depression; I of the 1980s. But there's something warm about reading the stories of others as they were growing up—especially if they share fond memories.

Some of Hastings' stories made me smile. He recalled how at Christmas every year, his father would kill one of their chickens. His mom would dress it, dry it, and package it. His dad then took the chicken to the post office and mailed it to their daughter in St. Louis.

"We sent what we could, and I always sensed that the package was tied by cords of love," Hastings wrote.

Reading Hastings' childhood stories made me appreciate the fact that over the next few years, I'll be largely responsible for making memories for my own children. Those memories will accompany them throughout their lives.

Will the thoughts they have fifty years from now make them smile? I'm fairly confident that their memories will never be as bitter as the woman who wrote her mother's obituary. But am I doing all I can to brighten their days and fill their lives with joy?

Too often I find myself tempted to shortchange my children to pursue my own selfish interests. Rather than playing with my children, it's easier for me to plop down and watch a ballgame or waste time on the computer.

The sad obituary carries a potent message for parents. What will our children say about us when we're gone?

I hope my children will never be tempted to say about me what this woman said about her mother: "There will be no service, no prayers, and no closure for the family she spent a lifetime tearing apart. We cannot come together in the end to see to it that her grandchildren and great-grandchildren can say their goodbyes. So I say here for all of us, GOOD BYE MOM."

-10-

From God's Word, the Bible...

Be anxious for nothing, but in everything by prayer and supplication, with thanksgiving, let your requests be made known to God; and the peace of God, which surpasses all understanding, will guard your hearts and minds through Christ Jesus.

Philippians 4:6-7

The Fretful Clock

(A Reading from Roger)

A woman was having trouble with her old clock. It seems that the clock had become anxious and upset. So the woman took the clock to a clock counselor.

"Old clock," said the counselor, "what is bothering you?"

And the clock responded: "I've been thinking about all the ticking I have to do! That's 2 ticks per second, 120 ticks per minute, 7,200 ticks per hour, 172,800 ticks per day, 1,209,600 ticks per week and 62,899,200 ticks per year. And the more I think, the more upset I become. What if I can't get all that ticking done?"

The counselor wisely asked: "How many ticks do you have to tick at a time?"

And the clock said: "Just one tick at a time."

So the counselor said: "Then tick one tick at a time. Don't even think about the next tick, till you get this tick ticked."

With that advice in hand, the woman took the old clock home and set it on the mantel. And it has been calmly ticking along ever since.

It seems to be a silly story. Clocks don't get anxious. They don't worry about all their ticking, and they don't go to see counselors. But we do. And this imaginative bit about the clock is designed to get us to see ourselves. We are the silly ones, filled with anxious days and hurried ways, throwing away the delights of today in our dithering about tomorrow. It is a bad, mad bargain. We can't tick today because we know we will have to tick tomorrow. Far too many can say:

*I worry about tomorrow, I fret over the past.
Meanwhile, today is leaving me fast.*

Are we to think about tomorrow and make wise preparations for it? Yes, of course. But that is different from being anxious and worried about it.

Jesus sees us—just as He so perfectly saw the members of His audience on the day that He delivered the Sermon on the Mount. An anxious lot they were, fretting over the future. Would they be able to find clothes to wear and food to eat? They were feeling the tyranny of tomorrow.

Jesus called their attention to the birds. Small, helpless creatures in a world of dangers, they would seem to be anxious. But they are content and happy.

Jesus also pointed them to the lilies, that is, to the wildflowers that were growing in the fields without any cultivation. He essentially said to His disciples (and to others): "Become disciples of those flowers. Learn from them."

The lesson they were to draw from those flowers was this: By using the means God had established for them, the lilies are adequately sustained for the time that God has appointed for them.

If God adequately sustains the lilies for the time He has appointed for them, we may be sure that He will sustain His people for the time He has appointed for them. How can we be sure? Because God's people are far more important to Him than flowers! And how do we know that? Let the Apostle Paul answer: "He who did not spare His own Son, but delivered Him up for us all, how shall He not with Him also freely give us all things?" (Rom. 8:32).

The cross of Christ, not our circumstances, is ever the key to understanding how God feels about His people.

So the cure for fretful living is to trust God to do what is best for us. Does this mean we will never experience anything that is unpleasant? Not at all! What is best for us is to be weaned away from this world so we will seek first God's kingdom and righteousness (Matt. 6:33). That requires the Lord to take an entirely different approach with us than He would if He were concerned only about our comfort and convenience.

The key to living in this world is to not live for this world but rather to live for a higher and better world. We are called to check our priorities each day to make sure we are living for that world and then to actually live for it—one tick at a time.

-11-

From God's Word, the Bible...

Take heed that you do not do your charitable deeds before men, to be seen by them. Otherwise you have no reward from your Father in heaven. Therefore, when you do a charitable deed, do not sound a trumpet before you as the hypocrites do in the synagogues and in the streets, that they may have glory from men. Assuredly, I say to you, they have their reward. But when you do a charitable deed, do not let your left hand know what your right hand is doing, that your charitable deed may be in secret; and your Father who sees in secret will Himself reward you openly.
Matthew 6:1-4

He who is faithful in what is least is faithful also in much; and he who is unjust in what is least is unjust also in much.
Luke 16:10

Unsung Heroes

(A Reading from Sylvia)

A local television station has a weekly feature called *Unsung Heroes* which highlights individuals who are doing something to benefit others in their sphere of influence. These individuals are not seeking recognition or praise for their deeds. They simply have a servant heart that desires to help others.

The kingdom of God also has many unsung heroes. They are followers of Christ who serve God faithfully in small churches and villages around the world. They are hidden from the world's eyes, but not from God's eyes.

In his book, *To the Golden Shore*, Courtney Anderson details an account of young Adoniram Judson's struggle as to what direction his life would take. He had a desire and drive to achieve greatness and fame, perhaps as the pastor of a great church in a large city where he would have praise and thousands would come to hear him preach.

> Without realizing how it happened, he found himself comparing this minister with an obscure country pastor, humbly striving only to bring his congregation and himself to God, without any thought of self. The minister in whose place he had imagined himself was really no better than any other ambitious man, anxious only for fame.
>
> What would the judgment be on him in the next world? If he achieved heaven, he would certainly not achieve fame in heaven. It would be the obscure country pastor whose fame would ring out there through eternity, even though he were never heard of here.[2]

When I read these words, I immediately thought of our son who has for years been pastor of a small, rural church. He labors diligently in the Word and doctrine (1 Tim. 5:17) to instruct and feed his small flock. And he is only one of many such pastors who serve faithfully in obscurity.

There are also vast numbers of unknown laymen who serve Christ their whole lives in their obscure little churches. They faithfully attend the worship services, give their tithe, pray, and minister in Christ's name to needs they see around them. They never achieve the world's fame, but they bring glory to God and advance His kingdom.

I thought of James and Katheryn Williams in the little country church where I grew up. They lived across the road from the church and were always present at every service. James did not become a Christian until he was a young adult, and although he was limited in education and shy by nature, he still found ways to serve the Lord. God had given him a powerful singing voice--and sing he did even though he could not read a note of music. For over forty years he led the congregation in singing the great hymns of the faith.

---

[2] To the Golden Shore: The Life of Adoniram Judson, Judson Press, Valley Forge, 1987, p.29

Katheryn led a girls' mission group, taught Sunday School, served as church clerk, taught in Vacation Bible School, and helped wherever else there was a need. Together James and Katheryn served as church custodians seeing to it that God's house was clean and in good condition. They are both now in the presence of the God they served so faithfully and obscurely in that little country church. But their legacy continues as their daughter, Peggy, has followed in their footsteps. Among other areas of service, Peggy has served faithfully as pianist in that same church for forty years—and counting.

God's view of heroes is far different from the world's. The world's heroes are often entertainers, athletes, and people in the public eye. God's heroes are those who have been faithful to serve Him where He has placed them, however obscure of a place that may be, and with the abilities He has given them, however limited those abilities may be. "Moreover it is required in stewards that one be found faithful" (1 Cor. 4:2). Those who have served God in obscurity will one day be rewarded openly (Matt. 6:4).

One of the joys of heaven will be to meet and learn about all the unsung heroes, the saints of God who faithfully served the Master in unknown places. Great will be their reward in heaven.

-12-

From God's Word, the Bible...

"Now therefore, listen to me, my children,
For blessed are those who keep my ways.
Hear instruction and be wise,
And do not disdain it.
Blessed is the man who listens to me,
Watching daily at my gates,
Waiting at the posts of my doors.
For whoever finds me finds life,
And obtains favor from the LORD;
But he who sins against me wrongs his own soul;
All those who hate me love death."

Proverbs 8:32-36

Wisdom for the Life Business

(A Reading from Roger)

We are all in the "life" business, and this is challenging business indeed. The bad news about this business is that it is very easy to mess it up. Many make life harder than it needs to be. They make poor choices, and poor choices lead to painful consequences. Poor choices sometimes bring life to an early end. In other cases, they can cause us to live with pain and heartache for years and years.

The Book of Proverbs is about the life business. It tells us what we can do to make life less challenging and more rewarding. Its message in one word? Wisdom! We have to be wise to master the life business. What is wisdom? It is knowing how to live. It is seeing and doing the right thing in the situations that life presents. It is essentially insight. It is making the right choices in life, choices that enable us to reap the good that life has to offer us.

If we live wisely, we will reap the good life has to offer. A little boy, trying to pick out a puppy, saw one wagging his tail, and said: "I want the one with the happy ending."

Making wise choices in life enables us to be happy at the end of the situation for which we are choosing. It should be obvious, then, that nothing is more important than getting wisdom (Prov. 4:7).

In Proverbs 8:32-36, the author steps aside, as it were, and allows wisdom herself to speak directly to us. And what does she have to say? The first thing is a command. She commands us to listen to her (v. 32).

She is offering us her services, but her offer will not help us if we refuse to listen! It's interesting that she refers to us as her "children." We should not take this as a compliment! Children are notorious for not listening! Children are, of course, very limited in knowledge. They rush ahead without thinking. They are easily deceived. They often refuse to exert the diligence that is necessary to learn. They prefer entertainment and excitement to learning. All of these traits are found in many adults when it comes to the matter of wisdom for living.

As wisdom continues to speak, she tells us what is necessary for listening—effort!

She pictures herself as living in a house. Each day she comes out of her front door and speaks to those who are waiting outside. Those who make the effort to be at her house reap the benefit of hearing her. They get insights on how to live. And it requires effort on their part! In order to be at wisdom's gates, one has to get up out of his bed, get dressed, make the journey to wisdom's house, and wait for her to appear.

How should we relate this to ourselves? The voice of wisdom speaks to us in the Bible. What must we do to hear her voice? We must read the Bible, hear it preached and taught, read good books about it, discuss it with others, and try to memorize key verses. Sadly enough, many people want the life skills that the Bible offers without having to put forth the effort to get them!

Finally, wisdom tells us the result of listening and the result of refusing to listen. The result of listening is blessing, which is a favor or benefit from God (vv. 32, 35). The result of not listening is calamity (v. 36).

There are temporal blessings for those who heed the voice of wisdom: longer life (3:2; 9:11; 10:2), peace of mind (3:2), favor with God and man (3:4; 12:2), direction (3:6), physical well-being (3:8), material well-being (3:10), happiness (3:13), stability (12:3).

But the greatest of all the blessings offered by wisdom is spiritual life here and now, and eternal life in the future. The Bible constantly sets the way of life and the way of death before us. The voice of wisdom urges us to choose life by trusting in the Lord Jesus Christ and His redeeming work.

Those who reject the voice of wisdom in the gospel "wrong" their souls and "love death" (v. 36).

-13-

From God's Word, the Bible...

Listen, O daughter,
Consider and incline your ear;
Forget your own people also, and your father's house;
So the King will greatly desire your beauty;
Because He is your Lord, worship Him.
And the daughter of Tyre will come with a gift;
The rich among the people will seek your favor.

Psalm 45:10-12
(Read the whole of Psalm 45 for this meditation.)

Words to the Bride

(A Reading from Martyn)

Psalm 45 is a celebration of a royal wedding. Like many of the Psalms it looks beyond the immediate circumstances that accompanied its writing and anticipates the glories of Jesus Christ.

The Bible frequently uses the imagery of a bridegroom and a bride to picture the relationship between Christ and His church. We are on solid ground in interpreting this Psalm as an anticipation of the wedding between Christ and His bride, the church. There are some words spoken to the bride in verses 10 to 12. They are words of exhortation and reassurance.

The first word of exhortation is "Forget" (v. 10). The bride is told to forget her own people and her father's house. It is not that she is to forget her family and her people in an absolute sense. The idea is that she is to be so thrilled by her husband that she does not long for her old life. The same exhortation is to be given to Jesus' bride, the church. We are to forget our old life. We are to leave it behind and cling to our Beloved (see Matt. 10:37 and Luke 14:26). Having been united to Christ, we are not to pine after the world and long for its company and its pleasures.

The second word of exhortation is "Worship" (v. 11). The bride of Christ is to honor and worship her Lord. Jesus is the sovereign Lord over all things, and all people owe Him worship. For His bride, it is a delight to obey this exhortation. As a wife finds it a delight to honor the husband whom she highly respects, so the church delights to worship her Husband, whose glories are described in the first nine verses of this psalm.

These verses also contain two words of assurance. Brides may at times have doubts. They may be in need of reassurance. So it is with the church. We sometimes struggle with doubts. Thankfully, there is much in God's Word to reassure us.

The first word of assurance is "The King desires you" (v. 11). One of the doubts that might trouble a bride is that her husband may not be pleased with her. The bride in this psalm is told there is no cause for such doubts. She is assured that the King will "greatly desire" her beauty. God's people know something about these doubts. Jesus' bride can think of endless reasons to be enthralled by His beauty but not a single reason why He should desire her. But God's Word assures us that Jesus greatly desires His bride. He takes pleasure in her not because she is beautiful in and of herself. Her beauty is all from Him. He has beautified her as an act of His grace and for His glory.

What a blessed thing it is to read in God's Word the reassuring words of Jesus' love for His own! The Bible tells us Jesus loves His bride and died for her. His thoughts for her cannot be numbered. He will return for her and draw her to His side. Nothing will ever separate her from His love. What blessed assurances these are!

The second word of assurance is "The nations will honor you" (v. 12). The idea in this verse is that people of high rank and great wealth from other nations will honor the King and His bride. Because of her closeness to the King, the bride will be honored and her favor will be sought.

Today, wherever the gospel triumphs among the nations, the bride of Christ is loved and honored. Wherever the King is worshiped, His queen is held in high regard. In this life, the people of God are hated, despised, and persecuted. But God's Word assures us that when Jesus returns He will vindicate His people. Before all creation, He will own His bride as His and see to it that she is honored.

How glorious is the Bridegroom and what glories await the Bride! Draw comfort from these assurances and heed the exhortations to forget and worship!

-14-

From God's Word, the Bible...

And as day was about to dawn, Paul implored them all to take food, saying, "Today is the fourteenth day you have waited and continued without food, and eaten nothing. Therefore I urge you to take nourishment, for this is for your survival, since not a hair will fall from the head of any of you." And when he had said these things, he took bread and gave thanks to God in the presence of them all; and when he had broken it he began to eat. Then they were all encouraged, and also took food themselves.

Acts 27:33-36

The Therapy of Thanks in the Thick of Things

(A Reading from Roger)

In Acts 27 we find the Apostle Paul "in the thick of things." You know what I mean by the thick of things: serious trouble or dire circumstances! I wonder if the phrase is an offshoot of "the thick of battle," which refers to that part of battle in which the heaviest fighting occurs.

But back to Paul; a prisoner of the Roman government, he was sailing to Rome to stand trial before Caesar (Acts 26:32). The charge leveled against him was sedition, that is, the inciting of rebellion against the government (Acts 24:5-6).

That would seem to be trouble enough. But Paul's trouble was only beginning. His ship encountered a "tempestuous head wind," which was called "Euroclydon," that is, a northeasterly wind.

This storm was so severe, that Luke, the author of Acts, says: "... we were exceedingly tempest-tossed" (v. 18), and "... no small tempest beat on us" (v. 20).

To make things worse, this storm continued for several days, two weeks to be exact! (v. 33).

The sailors had given up all hope. But in the midst of their despair, Paul came to offer encouragement and hope. One of the ways in which he did this was by giving them food.

Now here is a remarkable thing—in that setting of crisis, fear, confusion and exhaustion, Paul did not merely offer food. He first "gave thanks to God in the presence of them all" (v. 35).

If there has ever been a time in which the giving of thanks might seem to be out of place, this was it!

Paul could have said: "The men are preoccupied with the storm. There is no point in giving thanks." Or he could have said: "The men are in no mood to have religion crammed down their throats." Or he could have said: "The men will think I am crazy to thank God for food with this storm going on. Why thank God for the food when He won't stop the storm?"

But Paul expressed thanks just the same. It was a situation that would seem to call for bitterness, anger and skepticism, but Paul used it as an occasion for thanksgiving.

Why did he do it? Some would say it was mere force of habit, that Paul was observing his routine without thinking. That won't work. Paul was far too thoughtful, far too devoted to Christ, and far too genuine than to do this out of habit. This was a sincere expression of worship to God.

By doing this, Paul was declaring his conviction that God is with us in every situation. There would be no need to pray if God were not there to hear the prayer.

Paul was also registering his firm belief that every good

thing comes from God, even something as common as food, and that we owe thanks to Him. We must be thankful for the big things (v. 24), but we must not think that we exhaust our responsibility in so doing. We must also be thankful for the small things. By the way, if we are always thankful for small blessings, we will never fail to be thankful for large blessings.

Paul was also showing his companions that we are blessed even while we are burdened.

And what resulted from Paul's simple act of thanksgiving? Luke says "… they were all encouraged …" (v. 36).

Thankfulness never fails to leave a favorable impression. Sourness also leaves an impression but never a favorable one.

So let's make up our minds that we can go through life humbly grateful or grumbly hateful, and let's make it our business to choose the former.

With all his difficulties Paul was a grateful man. Do you wonder what he would say if he were asked to name the thing for which he was most grateful? I think he would say: "Thanks be to God for His indescribable gift" (2 Cor. 8:9). That gift, of course, is Christ and the eternal life we can receive through Him.

Be grateful for all God's gifts, and don't ever fail to be grateful for the greatest of His gifts.

-15-

From God's Word, the Bible...

Confess your trespasses to one another, and pray for one another, that you may be healed. The effective, fervent prayer of a righteous man avails much. Elijah was a man with a nature like ours, and he prayed earnestly that it would not rain; and it did not rain on the land for three years and six months. And he prayed again, and the heaven gave rain, and the earth produced its fruit.

James 5:16-18

I Want to Hear Bert Wilson Pray Again

(A Reading from Roger)

Before I began serving as a pastor (at age sixteen), I was a member of Vanburensburg Baptist Church in Vanburensburg, Illinois. It is likely that there are more letters in the church's name than there were members of the church.

One of the members was Bert Wilson. When I first got acquainted with Bert, he was already well advanced in years. I remember him as being very warm, kind, and humble.

The thing I remember most about Bert was his praying. Our dear pastor, Ernest Flowers—himself a wonderful Christian man—would often call on Bert to lead the congregation in prayer.

Our little church did not have pews. We had what we called theater seats. But they weren't plush, cushioned seats. They had wooden backs and wooden seats, and when we got up the seats would make a rather loud clacking noise. When the pastor called on Bert to pray, those seats would clack as members across the tiny building rose, not to stand during the prayer, but rather to kneel on the hardwood floor.

Everyone knew what to expect when Bert led in prayer. It would not be brief, light, and breezy. It would last from ten to fifteen minutes, and it would be earnest, heartfelt, and moving. It taught me that there is such a thing as laying hold of God in prayer. By the way, in the four or five years that I was a member of that church, I never heard anyone complain about the time Bert took to pray. If there had been any complaints about Bert's praying, I think they would have been along the lines of it being too brief. How that man prayed! And how time seemed to stand still when he prayed! Many in the congregation would find themselves lost in wonder, love, and praise when Bert prayed, and it was not at all unusual to hear people weeping during the prayer and to see tear-stained cheeks when it was over.

Bert was short in physical stature, but he was a spiritual giant. His prayers reminded us of the sovereignty and majesty of God and of His marvelous saving love—love that sent His Son to die on the cross for a world of unlovely, unworthy, undeserving sinners.

The trend in churches in recent years has been running against Bert Wilson. He would undoubtedly be told that prayer can't take too much time and can't be quite so serious. It seems these days that we are bent on making God small and casual. We dress casually, we pray casually, we preach casually, and we hurry to get through. The God of our day is smiling, benign, and user-friendly. His primary purpose seems to be to help us cope with life's difficulties and to manage our busy schedules. After it is all over, we might allow ourselves in an infrequent moment of deep reflection to wonder why God doesn't thrill our souls. We should not expect to get a big thrill from a little God. If we insist on making God little, we will get little in return. Bert prayed to a big God.

Serious times call for serious praying. These are serious times. Where are those who are seriously praying?

I am not Bert Wilson's equal in praying. My praying must sound in God's ears like the babbling of an infant compared to Bert's. But I do pray, and one of my prayers these days is this: Lord give us more Bert Wilsons.

I have many precious memories from my youth, but if someone were to ask me to choose one thing to relive, I think I would say: I want to hear Bert Wilson pray again.

-16-

From God's Word, the Bible...

"For the kingdom of heaven is like a man traveling to a far country, who called his own servants and delivered his goods to them. And to one he gave five talents, to another two, and to another one, to each according to his own ability; and immediately he went on a journey. Then he who had received the five talents went and traded with them, and made another five talents. And likewise he who had received two gained two more also. But he who had received one went and dug in the ground, and hid his lord's money. After a long time the lord of those servants came and settled accounts with them."

Matthew 25:14-19
(Read Matthew 25:14-30 for this meditation.)

Hard Thoughts About God

(A Reading from Martyn)

Jesus told the Parable of the Talents in Matthew 25:14-30. The first two servants in the parable made use of what their master entrusted to them and earned more talents for him. The third servant hid his master's money in the ground. When called to account, he defended his actions by saying, "Lord, I knew you to be a hard man."

There are many like the servant in this parable who have hard thoughts about God.

Many people perceive God to be harsh and demanding. When some think of God they believe Him to be exclusively a Lawgiver and a Judge. He is one who makes constant demands of us and who can never be pleased. This was Martin Luther's view of God before his glorious conversion.

Many think of God as one whose requirements of us far outweigh and surpass His gifts to us. They consider Him to be like Pharaoh who withheld straw from the Hebrews but still required them to produce the same number of bricks.

Another "hard thought" a lot of people have is that God is quick to punish and slow to reward. There are those who think that God is not only severe in making demands upon us, but that He is also eager to punish us when we sin. Those who view God this way will find no joy in serving Him. Serving Him will be a burdensome duty motivated by fear and not love.

Another "hard thought" of God held by many is that He is distant and joyless. There are some who perceive God to be like the typical father in Victorian England. He is distant from the child and demanding of the child. The child knows him only as a strict disciplinarian. There is no sharing of joy and laughter between father and child. There is only distance and coldness.

As God's people, we must beware of holding such hard thoughts about God. It is true that God is our Lawgiver and Judge. It is true that His Law makes demands upon us. But we must never forget that God is bountiful and generous, and pours out blessings upon us. The servant in this parable accused the master of expecting to reap where he has not sown. In pouring out His goodness, God does just the opposite. He sows kindness and blessings where He reaps no praise, thanks, or worship in return. He fills sinners with food who never thank Him for it. He gives life and breath to many who despise Him. How good God is!

Contrary to the hard thoughts about Him, God delights in rewarding His people. He does not forget faithful service rendered to Him, and it is His delight to reward His people for their obedience. The great marvel is that we would not obey God or perform any acts for His glory apart from Him working in us. So He grants us grace to obey Him and then graciously rewards our obedience. Oh, the goodness of God!

In his commentary on this passage, Alexander Maclaren wrote:

> My heart says to me many a time, "God's laws are hard; God's judgment is strict. God requires what you cannot give. Crouch before Him and be afraid." And my faith says, "Get thee behind me, Satan! He that spared not His own Son...how shall He not with Him also freely give us all things?" The cross of Christ is the answer to the slander of the giving God.[3]

The Bible also makes it clear that God is not like a distant, emotionless father. Rather, His heart is full of warmth, love, and joy. There is no joy like God's, and He loves to give expression to His joy. He desires for His people to be near Him and to share in His joy for all eternity.

Child of God, are you guilty of thinking your Father in heaven to be harsh and severe? Have you lost your joy in serving Him? Do you view Him as more of a taskmaster than a joyful Father who loves to be with His children? Meditate on the goodness, the kindness, the joy, the love of God. Ponder again the cross of Christ and delight yourself in the Lord and in His service!

---

[3] Alexander Maclaren, Expositions of Holy Scripture: St Matthew, Chaps. XVIII to XXVIII, Baker Book House, Grand Rapids, MI, 1974, p. 209.

-17-

From God's Word, the Bible...

...Grow in the grace and knowledge of our Lord and Savior Jesus Christ. To Him be the glory both now and forever.
Amen.

2 Peter 3:18

My Sanctified Dog, Gus

(A Reading from Tim)

I miss our morning conversations the most. Every morning I would go outside to see my dogs. While they were both happy to see me, Gus expressed his joy in a much more vocal way. It was almost as if he were singing to me with a "roo, roo, roo" type of sound that must have annoyed the neighbors. Sometimes I had to go back into the house just to get him to stop.

He was always thrilled to see me at any time of the day, but only in the mornings was I greeted in such a raucous manner. I came to call it my morning conversation with Gus. It was like he had been waiting all night to see me, and he simply wanted to tell my how his night had been.

I got Gus when he was just a puppy, probably only about three weeks old. He and his momma, who was half golden retriever, were residents of the local dog pound when I came in looking for two dogs to replace those we had just lost.

Gus was the only pup to survive from her litter of seven, and I took both him and his mom.

Gus (whom we named after the great Christian thinker Augustine) was a tiny little guy, fitting in the palm of my hand. He was entirely dependent upon his mother, Suzy, and when she would walk off and leave him behind, he would sit down, throw back his head, and let loose with a mournful cry. You would think his world had come to an end because his mom was a few yards away. He eventually grew to be almost twice her size, but he never stopped being her pup.

My mornings are a lot quieter now. At eleven years of age, Gus had been dealing with arthritis in his legs for some time. His condition had steadily worsened despite an increase in the pain-killing medication he was taking. It got to the place where he could hardly walk.

So we had to say goodbye. I knew for weeks that the day was coming and tried to prepare myself as best as I could. But it was still terribly difficult. He was my good and faithful friend, and a kind and gentle soul.

Through the pain he experienced late in life, Gus demonstrated to me what I grew to love most about him. The older he got and the more his legs hurt, the sweeter his disposition became. No one would have blamed him for being grumpy and sour, but that wasn't how Gus reacted. He simply loved us more and was all the more cheerful about life. Maybe he knew his days were numbered, and he wanted to make those days count.

It's probably not possible for a dog to be godly and to grow in sanctification. But all the same, Gus showed me what I must aspire to be like as I get older. Assuming that I live for at least a few more years, I'll most likely have to deal with a variety of aches and pains. Most people do. And many of them don't adjust very well. They become cranky and grouchy, and seem to take no enjoyment in their remaining days.

Gus wasn't that way at all. Just the opposite! Even until the day of his death, he was a jolly, loving, and sweet fellow, perhaps more so than he had ever been. I hope the same will one day be said of me—that as I approached death, my life reflected Christ more than ever before.

My mornings may be quieter without Gus, and I certainly miss his daily greeting. But maybe the silence will give me the opportunity to ponder the lessons he taught me and to ask myself if I'm growing in grace and love for the Lord and for His people. I pray God would make it so.

025 # -18-

From God's Word, the Bible...

Bow down Your ear, O LORD, hear me;
For I am poor and needy.

Psalm 86:1

Our Need-Meeting God

(A Reading from Sylvia)

We are a needy people. We have physical needs. We need oxygen every minute we live. We need food and water to sustain us. We also have emotional needs such as the need for love and acceptance. As believers in Jesus Christ we know about spiritual needs. We need a Savior who has forgiven our sins and given us His righteousness. We need God's grace and strength to face the trials of this life.

Even though we are a very needy people, we are not always conscious of our needs. But when difficulties and trials come our way we realize how needy we are, and how much we need God's help.

This was driven home to our family when our five-year-old grandson, Noah, was diagnosed with leukemia. We became keenly aware of our neediness. We needed God's healing grace for Noah. His parents needed wisdom for many decisions that suddenly had to be made. They desperately needed God's strength and peace to deal with their young child's suffering and the realization that he was facing three years of treatments with ugly side effects. Noah's two older siblings were needy as well. They needed understanding and patience to deal with the upheaval this journey would bring to their lives.

And then there was little Noah and his great needs. Yes, he needed healing. But in order for that healing to come about, he needed an abundant measure of courage and strength to face three years of needles, medical procedures, and the horrible side effects of the poisonous chemotherapy drug surging through his small body. How could one so young deal with all this—so much of which he could not even understand?

The answer to that question came early in Noah's leukemia journey. After two weeks of in-patient care at St. Jude Children's Hospital followed by several weeks of living in Memphis, Tennessee, to be near the hospital for daily out-patient treatments, Noah was able to return home.

Then began the hour-and-fifteen-minute weekly trips from home to St. Jude for blood work, doctor visits, and chemo treatments. Early in the routine of one of those Monday trips as our daughter-in-law was driving, she heard singing coming from the back seat. She listened closely to hear five-year-old Noah singing:

> *I need Thee, O I need Thee;*
> *Every hour I need Thee!*
> *O bless me now, my Savior,*
> *I come to Thee.*

Even at such a young age Noah seemed to realize his need for God's help. That was the answer to the question of how one so young and so needy could deal with this difficult journey that had been thrust upon him. And God in His grace met Noah's need. The treatments resulted in a cure for Noah. And with God's help, Noah faced his three-year-ordeal with amazing courage and strength, as did his parents and siblings.

Yes, we are indeed a needy people. But we have a need-meeting God. All thanks and praise to Him for meeting our greatest need—a Savior who provided payment for our sins so we can someday stand clean before a holy God. But thanks be to God also for meeting the many needs we have while living life in this world, and for the reminder of that coming from a five-year-old needy child.

-19-

From God's Word, the Bible...

Bless the LORD, O my soul;
And all that is within me, bless His holy name!
Bless the LORD, O my soul,
And forget not all His benefits:
Who forgives all your iniquities,
Who heals all your diseases,
Who redeems your life from destruction,
Who crowns you with lovingkindness and tender mercies,
Who satisfies your mouth with good things,
So that your youth is renewed like the eagle's.

Psalm 103:1-5
(Read the whole of Psalm 103 for this meditation.)

Who Like Me?

(A Reading from Martyn)

One of my favorite hymns is based on Psalm 103. It is entitled *Praise, My Soul, the King of Heaven*. The first stanza has these words:

> *Praise, my soul the King of heaven,*
> *to His feet your tribute bring;*
> *Ransomed, healed, restored, forgiven,*
> *who, like me His praise should sing?*
> *Praise Him, praise Him, praise Him, praise Him,*
> *Praise the everlasting King.*

The psalm upon which the hymn is based opens with these words:

> *Bless the LORD, O my soul;*
> *And all that is within me, bless His holy name!*
> *Bless the LORD, O my soul,*
> *And forget not all His benefits: …*
> (Psalm 103:1-2)

In the verses that follow David lists several of those benefits. That is also what the first stanza of the hymn does. It lists the benefits of being ransomed, healed, restored, forgiven. Let's consider each of these words.

The word *ransom* is similar to the word "redeem." It refers to being redeemed or delivered from sin by the payment of a price. The price that was paid for our redemption was nothing less than the blood of Jesus Christ (1 Peter 1:18-19). Psalm 103:4 reads, "Who redeems your life from destruction."

The next benefit is being *healed*. Psalm 103:3 says, "Who heals all your diseases."

Sin is a dreadful disease. It is far worse than any and all physical diseases. You would be better off to have Alzheimer's, Parkinson's, or have your body racked with cancer than to be still in the grip of sin. Sin is a terminal disease, and we are powerless to cure ourselves. The good news of the gospel is that there is healing for us in and through Jesus Christ. The miracles of physical healing He worked during His earthly ministry were meant to picture the far greater miracle of healing from the disease of sin.

The third benefit in the first stanza is being *restored*. In salvation God does a great work of restoration. He restores us to right standing with Him. He restores us to fellowship with Him. Through Christ we are reconciled to God and in Him God restores to us blessings lost in the fall and grants even greater blessings. Verse 5 of Psalm 103 says, "Who satisfies your mouth with good things, so that your youth is renewed like the eagle's." When we are saved, God restores us to a right relationship with Him, and then multiple times throughout our lives He restores and renews our strength.

The fourth benefit listed in the hymn is being *forgiven*. What a blessing this is! In Christ Jesus there is full pardon, complete forgiveness for all our sins, past, present, and future. Verse 3 of Psalm 103 says, "Who forgives all your iniquities." Verse 10 says, "He has not dealt with us according to our sins, nor punished us according to our iniquities." Verse 12 goes on to say, "As far as the east is from the west, so far has He removed our transgressions from us."

After listing these glorious benefits, the hymn writer goes on to ask, "Who like me His praise should sing?" In other words, he is saying since God has ransomed him, healed him, restored him, and forgiven him, he has great cause to praise God. Others who have been redeemed may have equal cause to praise God, but no one has greater cause to praise God. Do you believe that to be true of you, child of God? Do you believe that because of what Jesus has done for you, no one in this world has more cause to praise God than you?

A good practice for all Christians to learn is the discipline of talking to themselves. We ought to rehearse the truths of God's Word in our minds. That's what this hymn writer does. It is as if he found his soul in a cold condition and decided to give it a little coaching. He exhorts his own soul to praise the Lord. He rehearses the benefits God has bestowed upon him. He then asks his soul who should praise God more than he?

Consider memorizing this hymn and singing it on Sunday mornings as you prepare for worship. Let it be a help to you in talking to your soul and preparing yourself to praise and worship the Lord.

-20-

From God's Word, the Bible...

Your word I have hidden in my heart,
That I might not sin against You.
Blessed are You, O LORD!
Teach me Your statutes.
With my lips I have declared
All the judgments of Your mouth.
I have rejoiced in the way of Your testimonies,
As much as in all riches.
I will meditate on Your precepts,
And contemplate Your ways.
I will delight myself in Your statutes;
I will not forget Your word.

Psalm 119:11-16

Dad's Old Bible

(A Reading from Roger)

It's very old now, published in 1975. The pages are brown, and it has a musty smell. Some of the pages are loose. It is my Dad's Bible, a King James Version.

I have many Bibles. I have the KJV, NKJV, ESV, NASB, HCSB, NIV, the Amplified Bible, and the Living Bible. I have Study Bibles with all sorts of detailed notes and explanations. I have plain Bibles with nothing but the Bible books themselves and four or five maps in the back. I have expensive and inexpensive Bibles. I have large-print and regular-print Bibles. I have Bibles with black, burgundy, brown, and blue covers.

But no Bible is more precious to me than Dad's Bible. As I open it I find the page where he wrote his name.

It is somewhat surprising to me that my Dad was not much of a Bible marker. I am. I underline and write notes in the margin. I seem to recall someone, after looking at all the underlinings in my Bible, asking: "If you underline the whole Bible, how is it different from one that is not underlined at all?"

My Dad did underline a little. One of the few verses, interestingly enough, comes from the tiny prophecy of Obadiah: "But upon mount Zion shall be deliverance, and there shall be holiness; and the house of Jacob shall possess their possessions" (v. 17).

I'm not sure why that verse was so special to Dad. My guess is that it made him look forward to that glorious day in which the people of God will possess all that God has promised to give them.

One of the underlined verses in the New Testament is John 6:29—"Jesus answered and said unto them, This is the work of God, that ye believe on him whom he hath sent."

This verse points out the importance of believing in the Lord Jesus Christ. While still a young man, my father came to faith in Christ. He loved and served the Lord Jesus. It is no surprise that one of his underlined verses is Philippians 1:21—"For to me to live is Christ, and to die is gain."

Another verse he marked in Philippians is Paul's warning to rejoice in Christ and put no confidence in the flesh (Phil. 3:3).

One of the more heavily marked sections is in Paul's first letter to the Thessalonians: "For this we say unto you by the word of the Lord, that we which are alive and remain unto the coming of the Lord shall not prevent them which are asleep. For the Lord himself shall descend from heaven with a shout, with the voice of the archangel, and with the trump of God: and the dead in Christ shall rise first: Then we which are alive and remain shall be caught up together with them in the clouds to meet the Lord in the air: and so shall we ever be with the Lord" (1 Thess. 4:15-17).

Dad died on August 4, 1985. His body lies alongside my mother's in little Greenhill Cemetery, just outside Vanburensburg, Illinois. His soul is already with the Lord, and now his body waits for the sound of the trumpet, the voice of the archangel, and the shout of Jesus. That body will then spring from the grave, will be instantaneously changed into a body just like the resurrection body of Jesus (Phil. 3:21), will be re-joined to his soul, and he will soul and body be forever with the Lord.

How do I know these things to be true? They are all right there in Dad's old Bible.

> *Though the cover is worn*
> *And the pages are torn,*
> *And though places bear traces of tears,*
> *Yet more precious than gold*
> *Is the Book, worn and old,*
> *That can shatter and scatter my fears.*
>
> *When I prayerfully look*
> *In the precious old Book,*
> *Many pleasures and treasures I see;*
> *Many tokens of love*
> *From the Father above,*
> *Who is nearest and dearest to me.*
>
> *This old Book is my guide,*
> *This a friend by my side,*
> *It will lighten and brighten my way;*
> *And each promise I find*
> *Soothes and gladdens my mind*
> *As I read it and heed it today.*
> (Author unknown)

-21-

From God's Word, the Bible...

Thanks be to God for His indescribable gift!

2 Corinthians 9:15

Getting the "Hallelujah!" Back (1)

(A Reading from Roger)

When was the last time you let out a good hearty Hallelujah? For that matter, when was the last time you silently cried Hallelujah? The Hallelujah, along with the Amen, seems to have been carried off and buried in the cemetery of good Christian words. Did it die from lack of use?

The word Hallelujah, meaning "God be praised," is a word that was intended to express the thrill believers get from their God. It could be used in reference to all the works and wonders of God, but it is never more fitting than when it is used in connection with the redeeming death of the Lord Jesus Christ.

Philip Bliss used the word in the highest and best way:

*"Man of sorrows," what a name, For the Son of God who came
Ruined sinners to reclaim! Hallelujah! What a Savior!*

*Bearing shame and scoffing rude, In my place condemned He stood,
Seal'd my pardon with His blood; Hallelujah! What a Savior!*

*Lifted up was He to die, "It is finished," was His cry,
Now in heav'n exalted high, Hallelujah! What a Savior!*

*When He comes, our glorious King, All His ransomed home to bring,
Then anew this song we'll sing, Hallelujah! What a Savior!*

What will it take for the church to get her Hallelujahs back? For one thing, she must think deeply again about Bliss' phrase "ruined sinners." No one can ever truly rejoice in salvation until he has known himself to be a ruined sinner. To be a sinner is to stand guilty before the holy God. It is to be guilty of breaking His laws. And the "ruined" part? That means any chance of ever standing acceptably in the presence of God is gone—ruined! We are guilty sinners, and there is nothing we can do to remedy our situation.

On top of that the church must think in depth about those words "... the Son of God who came."

Here we are in our sins with no way of helping ourselves, but God did something for us. He sent His Son, the Lord Jesus, to this earth to "reclaim" sinners. Can it be that God could care enough for sinners to send His Son?

And getting "Hallelujah" back means thinking through what Jesus had to endure in order to save sinners. Bliss gets at a tiny portion of it in the phrase "bearing shame and scoffing rude." After He was taken into custody, the Lord Jesus had to bear the vilest mockery imaginable. Shame and scoffing were heaped upon Him. Then He was "lifted up" to die on the cross. Why did He endure all the shame and suffering? Let Bliss answer: "In my place condemned He stood."

Everything Jesus endured was that which sinners deserve to endure. Every evil thing that came His way came because He was standing in the place of sinners. He was their substitute.

Some theologians, preachers, and church members think it is necessary to wage war on the teaching of Christ as our substitute. Some even suggest that the future wellbeing of Christianity hangs on getting rid of the notion of substitution. But it is as simple as this: if you take the substitution of Christ out of Christianity, you no longer have Christianity. And you no longer have any possibility of salvation for sinners. If you need to be up to date, you will need to get rid of substitution. Let me hang on to it and be out of date.

Biblical Christianity, and, really, there is no other kind, can be reduced to these propositions:

- I deserve hell.
- Jesus took my hell.
- Now there is nothing left for me but heaven.

But what if we take out the second proposition? What if we say that Jesus did not take our hell when He was on the cross and cried: "My God, My God, why have You forsaken Me?" (Matt. 27:46).

Yes, what then? If we know ourselves to be deserving of hell and do not say that Jesus took it on our behalf, do we not have to say that we must take it ourselves?

If we let the substitution that Bliss advocated in his hymn really soak into our brains, we won't have to worry about the *Hallelujah, what a Savior* part. Let us truly understand salvation, and the *Hallelujah* will sound inwardly or outwardly or both.

-22-

From God's Word, the Bible...

Seek the LORD while He may be found,
Call upon Him while He is near.
Let the wicked forsake his way,
And the unrighteous man his thoughts;
Let him return to the LORD,
And He will have mercy on him;
And to our God,
For He will abundantly pardon.

Isaiah 55:6-7

Getting the "Hallelujah!" Back (2)

(A Reading from Roger)

We're trying to find our way back to the word "Hallelujah," and we are doing so by looking at a well-known hymn from the pen of Philip Bliss. It can be found in some hymnals under the title *Man of Sorrows* and in others with the title *Hallelujah! What a Savior!* The former asserts that Jesus fulfilled the prophecy of Isaiah 53:6. We should not think that Jesus was a miserable and unhappy man, but He could see here the terrible effects of sin and that brought sorrow to His heart. He was also here on the serious business of receiving the penalty for sinners.

If your Hallelujah has been silenced and stifled, you will find in Bliss' hymn plenty of words and phrases to get it revived.

What blessing there is in that word "pardon"! To be pardoned is to have the just sentence—the sentence that we deserved to receive—lifted. What is the sentence for our sins? It is eternal death. By shedding His blood, Jesus secured the pardon of all who believe. That blood represents His death, and the physical blood that poured out from Him on the cross represents Him receiving the full penalty for our sins.

Get a good look at that word "pardon." Walk around it a few times. Understand the reality of your sins and what Christ did on the cross for sinners, and let the Hallelujah ring in your heart.

And what blessing there is in these words: "'It is finished,' was His cry." What Jesus did on the cross perfectly and fully purchased our salvation. There is nothing for us to add to what He did. It is ours to merely receive by faith in Him and in the work He did. When you see the enormous problem posed by the salvation of sinners and you see that Jesus solved that problem, you will cry, "Hallelujah!"

The cross on which He died is, of course, not the final word about the Lord Jesus. He sprang from His grave in glorious resurrection life and ascended to the Father in heaven. He is back in heaven in exalted glory, the object of the praises of the angels. But He is not back in heaven now in the same way that He was before. He has carried the humanity that He took at Bethlehem back to heaven with Him. And the fact that He is there in resurrected humanity is the guarantee that all who believe in Him will follow Him into heaven in resurrected humanity. Now, that will make you shout, "Hallelujah! What a Savior!"

If Hallelujah is still fading in our hearts and dying on our tongues, we can surely get it back by savoring this verse:

When He comes, our glorious King, All His ransomed home to bring,
Then anew this song we'll sing, Hallelujah! what a Savior!

The Lord Jesus will return from heaven with a shout, the

voice of an archangel, and a blast from the trumpet of God. He will bring with Him the souls of all believers who have died, and He will raise their bodies from their graves. Those resurrected bodies will be rejoined to those souls, and those believers who are still alive will be instantaneously changed and caught up to meet the Lord in the air (1 Thess. 4:13-18).

From there the Lord Jesus will lead His people into the glory of a new heaven and a new earth (Rev. 21 and 22). There we will see the magnificent sweep of redemption's plan, and we will marvel at it all. We will be amazed and astounded beyond words at a plan that was born in eternity past in the mind and heart of the triune God, that caught us up as it swept through human history, and finally dropped us on heaven's shore. There our Hallelujahs will abound and will never diminish and never decrease.

In these days, many in the church are striving for relevance. In so doing, they are focusing on helping people cope with their problems and helping them manage the challenges of life. The question that ought to be pounding in our heads is this: in our quest to make Christianity relevant, have we made it small? We need not expect a small Christianity to thrill us. The hymn of Philip Bliss lets us see how big true Christianity is, and urges us when we have seen it to shout, "Hallelujah!"

-23-

From God's Word, the Bible...

For now we see in a mirror, dimly, but then face to face. Now I know in part, but then I shall know just as I also am known.
1 Corinthians 13:12

Therefore we do not lose heart. Even though our outward man is perishing, yet the inward man is being renewed day by day. For our light affliction, which is but for a moment, is working for us a far more exceeding and eternal weight of glory, while we do not look at the things which are seen, but at the things which are not seen. For the things which are seen are temporary, but the things which are not seen are eternal.
2 Corinthians 4:16-18

Seeing from Heaven's Glory with Heaven's Eyes

(A Reading from Sylvia)

In the small country church I attended in my childhood years, we often sang the hymn *Farther Along*.

This hymn, sometimes attributed to W.B. Stevens and sometimes to W.A. Fletcher, came to mean so very much to me because of a horrible tragedy in our community.

I was nine years old. I can still see the six caskets at the graveside service. The closed caskets were lined up from the largest to smallest. Inside the largest casket was the body of a mother. The next casket held the body of her teenage daughter, followed by four younger children. This mother and her five children had died in a house fire. They lived in the little community where my family attended church, and the children had sometimes attended our church.

The family was extremely poor. The husband and father

had abandoned the family so the mother was rearing the children with the help of her father who lived with them in their tiny house. The night of the fire, the grandfather and two boys, one of whom was my age, were able to escape the burning house. But the mother and the other five children perished in the fire.

I remember the perplexity of the godly people in my church family, including my parents. There were no words to express the depth of this tragedy and the sorrow it brought to all our hearts. It was so hard to understand why a family that had so much hardship had to come to such a tragic end. But there could be no understanding it—at least not in this life. But our faith in God assured us that we would understand by and by. So as people from our church and the community gathered in the cemetery that cold day in 1955, a group from our church sang these words:

> *Tempted and tried we're oft made to wonder*
> *Why it should be thus all the day long,*
> *While there are others living about us,*
> *Never molested, though in the wrong.*

> (Refrain)
> *Farther along we'll know all about it,*
> *Farther along we'll understand why;*
> *Cheer up my brother, live in the sunshine,*
> *We'll understand it all by and by.*

As verse two was sung I remember how I grieved for the surviving members of this family as I thought about how lonely and drear their future days would be.

> *When death has come and taken our loved ones*
> *It leaves our home so lonely and drear,*

> *Then do we wonder why others prosper*
> *Living so wicked year after year.*

The last verse and chorus was an expression of our hope in spite of our inability to understand:

> *When we see Jesus, coming in glory,*
> *When He comes from His home in the sky,*
> *Then we shall meet Him in that bright mansion,*
> *We'll understand it all by and by.*

Decades later, the scene of six caskets of descending size lined up in a cemetery has never left me. I have never heard *Farther Along* sung or played without that scene rushing back to my mind.

> *Farther along we'll know all about it,*
> *Farther along we'll understand why;*
> *Cheer up my brother, live in the sunshine,*
> *We'll understand it all by and by.*

God's people often yearn to have the tragedies of this life explained here and now, but we do not get all the explanations we desire. We must wait for that time in which we enter heaven's glory. Then we will see with heaven's eyes. And then, at last, we will understand. Farther along!

-24-

From God's Word, the Bible...

For He made Him who knew no sin to be sin for us, that we might become the righteousness of God in Him.

2 Corinthians 5:21

The New Dress

(A Reading from Sylvia)

It was a blue print, shirt-waist style dress that I can still picture decades later. But my mother's reaction to it took me completely by surprise. I was thirteen years old and had just returned from a trip to Texas. The trip was an eighth grade graduation present from my aunt.

My aunt and her daughter had previously lived in Texas where my uncle's family resided but had moved back home to Illinois after my uncle died. Now two years later they were taking a vacation trip to Texas to visit relatives and invited me to go along.

I had been given a little money by my parents to spend on the trip. I also had some graduation gift money and the money I had been saving for weeks in anticipation of this trip. Of course I would spend some of that on souvenirs for my parents and four younger brothers. It would be unthinkable to return home without bringing gifts for my family.

Once we arrived in Texas, every place we stopped had souvenirs for sale. I picked out inexpensive trinkets for my dad and brothers. But for my mother I had something different in mind. I wanted to buy her a dress.

My dad was a hardworking but struggling farmer. And with five children, there was barely enough money to provide the necessities. My mother, like most mothers, always sacrificed her own wants and often her needs in order to provide for her children. A new dress was a luxury Mother rarely allowed herself to enjoy. She always saw to it that I had a new dress for Easter, but that didn't leave any money for a new dress for her.

Assessing the amount of money I had to spend on this trip, I came up with a plan. If I would buy some inexpensive gifts for my dad and brothers and spent sparingly on myself, I would probably have enough money to buy Mom a dress. And that is exactly what I did. My aunt took me to a dress shop where I took my time looking at the dresses and finally picked out the dress that I thought would be perfect for Mom.

Upon my return home I proudly presented my family members with their gifts. My dad and brothers were pleased with their trinkets, but when my mother opened the box containing the dress she began to cry—tears of surprise and joy. I expected her to be pleased, but I had no idea she would react with such emotion. She wore the new dress to church the next Sunday and many Sundays afterward.

As I was thinking recently about this event from my childhood, I thought about another kind of dress—the robe of righteousness given to us when we receive Jesus Christ as our Lord and Savior. I recalled the words in Isaiah 61:10:

I will greatly rejoice in the LORD,
My soul shall be joyful in my God;
For He has clothed me with the garments of salvation,
He has covered me with the robe of righteousness...

How marvelous is this garment of salvation, the robe of righteousness. It has been provided as a free gift from God. In order to be acceptable to God we must be righteous, meaning perfect. Because we can never be perfect by our own efforts, our gracious God provided a righteousness for us through the Lord Jesus Christ.

This priceless gift of righteousness should bring great joy to us, not only when we are first saved, but throughout the rest of our lives. In fact the joy of our salvation should increase all the more as we grow spiritually and as our knowledge of the plan of redemption increases. Our joy will reach its pinnacle when we stand before God at the end of time, and in the words of Edward Mote we are

> *Dressed in His righteousness alone,*
> *Faultless to stand before the throne.*
> (From the hymn, *The Solid Rock*)

My mother's new dress eventually faded and wore out, but thank God our garment of salvation, the robe of righteousness, will never fade or wear out but will clothe us throughout eternity.

-25-

From God's Word, the Bible...

But God demonstrates His own love toward us, in that while we were still sinners, Christ died for us.

Romans 5:8

The Wonderful Cross

(A Reading from Roger)

The Apostle Paul was a cross-lover. He loved the cross of Christ. To him, the cross was the most wonderful thing in all of human history.

Do you understand Paul? Are you a cross-lover? If you were asked to name the one thing that is more wonderful to you than anything else, what would you say?

Every Christian loves the cross of Christ, but we all need to love it more.

I am asking you to think with me about that cross. In particular, I am asking you to think with me about this question: what makes the cross of Christ so wonderful?

My first answer to that question is this: it is wonderful because of the person who died there.

It isn't enough to merely say Jesus of Nazareth was on that cross. Nor is it enough to say a great teacher was there, or a great moral example was there.

You have never said enough about Jesus until you say He was God in human flesh. Someone has estimated that 60 billion people have occupied planet earth. The Lord Jesus can be described as 1 in 60 billion. I am saying that He is in a class by Himself. No one else is like Him—fully God, fully man—the God-man!

Are you wishing you could know the truth about Jesus? You can. These things tell you everything you need to know about Him:

- the prophecies He fulfilled
- the miracles He performed
- the words He spoke
- the lives He changed
- the grave He conquered

My second answer to that question is this: it is wonderful because of what He did there.

Jesus was not only a special person; He was on that cross to die a special death—a death such as no one before had ever died or anyone since.

It is never enough to think of Jesus' death in mere physical terms. Yes, He died physically, but there was much more to it than that.

Jesus was on that cross to receive the penalty for sinners. What is that penalty? It is eternal separation from God. Jesus bore that penalty. He experienced an eternity's worth of separation from God there. That's why He cried, "My God, My God, why have You forsaken Me?" (Matt. 27:46).

If you ask me how Jesus in the six hours He was on the cross could receive an eternity's worth of the wrath of God, I would say: because He was an infinite person, He could bear in a finite amount of time an infinite amount of wrath.

Paul, the cross-lover, says in Romans 3:25 that Jesus is the propitiation for our sins. That word propitiation means He appeased or satisfied the wrath of God on behalf of sinners.

Have you ever wondered why we tell people to trust in Jesus and what He did on the cross for their eternal salvation? The Romans crucified thousands of men. Why do we say look to this one man hanging on this one cross? It is because He was a special man dying a special kind of death.

Here is my final answer to that question: it is wonderful because of what put that special man there to do that special work.

The love of God put Jesus on that cross—the love of God for unworthy, undeserving sinners. Our calling is not to understand that love—it is far too great for that—but to rejoice in it and to worship the One who has loved us.

> *Could we with ink the ocean fill,*
> *And were the skies of parchment made,*
> *Were every stalk on earth a quill,*
> *And every man a scribe by trade;*
> *To write the love of God above*
> *Would drain the ocean dry;*
> *Nor could the scroll contain the whole,*
> *Tho' stretched from sky to sky.*

(Frederick M. Lehman, *The Love of God*)

-26-

From God's Word, the Bible...

Do not fret because of evildoers,
Nor be envious of the workers of iniquity.
For they shall soon be cut down like the grass,
And wither as the green herb.
Trust in the LORD, and do good;
Dwell in the land, and feed on His faithfulness.
Delight yourself also in the LORD,
And He shall give you the desires of your heart.

Psalm 37:1-4
(Read the whole of Psalm 37 for this meditation.)

God's Prescription for an Age-Old Malady

(A Reading from Martyn)

As we travel through this life there are times when our souls are afflicted by various maladies. One of the things that can lead us into a dark season of the soul is the fact that the wicked often prosper in this life. God's people seek to honor Him, yet we often seem to fail and have little to show for our efforts. The wicked, on the other hand, give no thought to God yet seem to always meet with success. They are often rich and prosperous. They often occupy positions of leadership and influence. This malady of being discouraged when the wicked prosper has been around a long time. It is still with us today.

In Psalm 37 God has a prescription to cure this malady. This prescription involves some things we must not do and some things we must do.

The first thing we must not do is fret (v. 1). We are not to get worked up and worry ourselves over the prosperity of the wicked. Even though the wicked prosper and bring their schemes to pass, we are not to fret over it.

The second thing we must not do is become envious (v. 1). The people of God should never desire to trade places with the wicked. Verse 2 tells us why we should not envy the wicked.

> *For they shall soon be cut down like the grass,*
> *And wither as the green herb.*

They may be prospering for now, but their prosperity will be short-lived.

The third thing we must not do is give way to anger and wrath (v. 8). When the wicked seem to be triumphing we must guard against becoming angry with God. Are you ever tempted to say in anger: "Why doesn't God do something about...?"

These verses also give us a positive side to this prescription. They tell us two things we must do.

First, we must look up. We must get our eyes off the godless and fix our eyes upon God. Verse 3 tells us to "Trust in the LORD." Trust Him and never forget that He is in control of all things. Verse 3 goes on to say, "and do good." Don't be taken up with what the wicked are doing. Be taken up with what God has given you to do. Verse 4 tells us to delight ourselves in the Lord. The energy spent worrying about the godless could better be spent delighting in God. We are further told in verse 7 to "rest in the LORD." Rest in knowing that every promise God has made about the triumph of His kingdom will be fulfilled. Wait patiently for God to act. Rest in knowing that the governing of all things is in the best possible hands.

Secondly, we must look ahead. We are to look to the future and know that a great change is coming. Verse 9 tells us, "evildoers shall be cut off; but those who wait on the LORD, they shall inherit the earth."

The same idea is expanded upon in verses 10 and 11. When you are tempted to despair over the prosperity of the wicked remember that phrase in verse 10, "for yet a little while." The wicked may seem to be having their day, but their time will soon come to an end. Look to the future and know that there will be no peace for the wicked, and there will be nothing but peace for the saints of God. When the wicked are gone and forgotten, the righteous will be forever enjoying the earth they have inherited and delighting themselves in the abundance of peace.

If you are afflicted by the malady of being discouraged by wicked people who seem to always succeed, read Psalm 37 and meditate deeply upon it. It is God's prescription for this age-old malady.

-27-

From God's Word, the Bible...

Then the word of the LORD came to Jeremiah, saying, "Behold, I am the LORD, the God of all flesh. Is there anything too hard for Me?"

Jeremiah 32:26-27
(Read the whole of Jeremiah 32 for this meditation.)

The Ups and Downs of Faith

(A Reading from Roger)

These were terrible days for the city of Jerusalem. She was surrounded by the Babylonian army. And they were terrible days for Jeremiah. He was in prison (v.2).

While Jeremiah was whiling away his time in jail, the Lord told him to expect a visit from his cousin Hanamel. Hanamel owned a field in nearby Anathoth, and he wanted to sell it to Jeremiah. Perhaps Hanamel had figured a way to get out of town, and he needed a little spending money.

The presence of the Babylonian army outside the city had caused all commerce to cease in Jerusalem. But Hanamel figured his weird cousin Jeremiah might take the field off his hands.

The Lord told Jeremiah to do exactly that, and Jeremiah did. He paid Hanamel the seventeen shekels he was asking for the field and had two deeds properly and legally prepared.

Here we see Jeremiah functioning as a child of God ought to function—in faith. He listened to God, believed God, and obeyed God.

This deal should have made sense to Jeremiah. He had been preaching two things for a long time: (1) the people of Jerusalem would be taken captive by the Babylonians; (2) after seventy years the people would be released from their captivity in Babylon (29.10,14; 30.8,10-11,18; 31.8,10,16-17,23-28)

So Jeremiah should have understood that in buying this field, he was providing something that his descendants could use. But he began to waver. He did not doubt the first part of his message. He believed the captivity would take place. As he looked out the window, he could see the Babylonian army!

But for some reason he seemed to doubt the second part of his message, namely, that the Jews would be released. So he began to question God. Why did God want him to act as if there was a future for the Jews when their circumstances seemed to suggest otherwise?

The Babylonians were so strong, and the Jews were so weak! Did it not make more sense to believe that the Babylonian captivity would be the final word for the Jews?

In the midst of his bout with doubt, Jeremiah did a very wise thing. He prayed! (v. 16). Let this be a lesson to us! When we have difficulties on every hand and our faith is weak, let us pray! Let us tell the Lord all about it! Matthew Henry says: "Prayer is the salve for every sore."

The Lord responded to Jeremiah's prayer of doubt. Here is the very first thing the Lord said to him: "Behold, I am the LORD, the God of all flesh. Is there anything too hard for Me?" (v. 26).

This question, Phillip Ryken suggests, contains "an ounce of rebuke and a pound of grace."

Yes, there is rebuke here. Knowing as he did about the greatness of God, Jeremiah should not have allowed himself to slip into doubt. But there is more grace here than rebuke. Any time the Lord reminds us of His greatness, He is being gracious to us.

God was promising two things regarding the people of Jerusalem: they would be taken captive to Babylon and they would eventually be restored to their land. In other words, God was promising both calamity and hope. Jeremiah did not doubt the calamity part. He could see the Babylonians outside the city. He did, however, doubt the hope part.

We are often like Jeremiah. In light of the greatness of our sins, it is often easier for us to believe that God will judge than that He will forgive. We find ourselves wondering how it's possible for a holy God to forgive such great sinners. God says the same to us that He said to Jeremiah: Nothing is impossible with Him. That includes forgiveness. Forgiveness for our sins might seem impossible to us, but God found a way. That way is His Son, Jesus, dying on the cross.

Let's come away from Jeremiah's experience asking ourselves:

- Do we believe God's Word even when it seems foolish to do so?
- Do we tell the Lord about our doubts and uncertainties?
- Do we really believe that nothing is impossible with God, even the forgiveness of our sins?

-28-

From God's Word, the Bible...

For our light affliction, which is but for a moment, is working for us a far more exceeding and eternal weight of glory, while we do not look at the things which are seen, but at the things which are not seen. For the things which are seen are temporary, but the things which are not seen are eternal.

2 Corinthians 4:17-18

Lord, Help Me to Spaffordize

(A Reading from Roger)

You've never heard the word "spaffordize"? There's a reason for that. I just now made it up. It is based on the name of a man who lived many years ago—Horatio G. Spafford. To "spaffordize," I suggest, is to respond to brutal circumstances the way he did.

The date was November 22, 1873. On its way to England, the ship *Ville du Havre* was struck by another vessel and sank. Many people—226—lost their lives, including the four young daughters of Horatio and Anna Spafford. Anna was also on the ship but survived. The loss of their daughters followed the death from scarlet fever of their four-year-old son two years earlier.

Upon learning of the tragedy, Spafford himself set sail for England to be with his wife. His voyage took him over the place where his daughters had died, and it gave him the occasion to write the hymn that has brought blessing to millions—*It is Well with My Soul*.

The words of this hymn are remarkable. There is no attempt here to deny or to soften the pain of the trial; quite the opposite! In his second line, Spafford acknowledges his crushing grief: "When sorrows like sea billows roll…"

The hymn powerfully affirms two truths in which every Christian can find refuge in the midst of the most heartbreaking trials.

The first truth is this: the greatness of the burden does not destroy the greatness of the blessing.

> *Though Satan should buffet, tho' trials should come,*
> *Let this blest assurance control,*
> *That Christ has regarded my helpless estate,*
> *And hath shed His own blood for my soul.*

The Christian may be broken, beaten, and battered, but he is also blessed. In the midst of the most trying circumstances, he can always say: "Yes, but…" He says "Yes" regarding the trial. Yes, it hurts. Yes, it breaks my heart. Yes, the tears flow. Yes, the questions abound. Then he adds the word "but"—but with it all I still enjoy the greatest of all possible blessings, that is, my salvation through Christ. No earthly ill, no matter how severe and heart-wrenching, can ever deprive me of that blessing. The things of this world—families, friends, health, possessions, pleasures—are not secure. Salvation through Christ is. So the believer can say: "It is well, it is well with my soul," and nothing can ever keep such a person from saying it. And it is not just a matter of saying it but rather rejoicing in it with worshipful amazement:

> *My sin—oh the bliss of this glorious thought!*
> *My sin, not in part but the whole,*

> *Is nail'd to the cross, and I bear it no more,*
> *Praise the Lord, praise the Lord, O my soul!*

And the second truth? It is this: a glorious day will come when all of our sorrows and suffering will end in magnificent victory:

> *And, Lord, haste the day when the faith shall be sight,*
> *The clouds be rolled back as a scroll,*
> *The trump shall resound and the Lord shall descend,*
> *"Even so," it is well with my soul.*

Now we walk by faith, and the eye of faith is dim. The Apostle Paul tells us that we now see through a glass "darkly" (1 Cor. 13:12, KJV). But when Jesus comes, the dark glass will be removed and we shall see "face to face," that is, with clarity. On that day we will understand the things that we found so perplexing and puzzling in this life, and all will make perfect sense. T.V. Moore says there is coming a "... great day of final adjustment ... in which all seeming anomalies of the present shall be fully explained and wholly removed forever."

Our faith doesn't enable us to see all that God is doing now, but it does enable us to see that coming day and to join Spafford in saying: "Lord, haste the day..."

Life may present you with many burdens and challenges. For me, the road has not been bump-free. But I have never had anything as crushing as what Horatio and Anna Spafford had to endure. Like yours, my journey is not complete. There may be significant hardships ahead. Whether our future problems be great or small, I pray the Lord will give grace to "spaffordize" by not letting my burdens—or your burdens—overshadow the blessing. Let us look beyond this vale of tears to that tearless day.

-29-

From God's Word, the Bible...

Deliver those who are drawn toward death,
And hold back those stumbling to the slaughter.
Proverbs 24:11

And He said to them, "Go into all the world and preach the gospel
to every creature.
Mark 16:15;

Brethren, my heart's desire and prayer to God for Israel is that they
may be saved…
"How beautiful are the feet of those who preach the gospel of peace,
Who bring glad tidings of good things!"
Romans 10:1, 15

Can You Bear to Let Them Go?

(A Reading from Sylvia)

At a worship service I recently attended we sang the hymn, *Brethren, We Have Met to Worship* written by George Atkins. Verse two of that hymn has these words:

> *Brethren, see poor sinners round you*
> *Slumbering on the brink of woe;*
> *Death is coming, hell is moving,*
> *Can you bear to let them go?*

Many Christians appear to be answering that question in the affirmative: "Yes, we can bear to let them go." Among believers today there seems to be little concern and thus little praying and pleading for the souls of unbelievers. But I vividly remember two members of my family who demonstrated by their actions that their answer was, "No, I cannot bear to let them go." One was my Grandma Tate.

When I was in high school, I stayed all night with Grandma almost every Thursday during the school year. Grandma lived just a mile or so from the small town where I attended high school. My family lived on a farm several miles from town. On Thursdays after school, instead of riding the bus home, I walked to the home of my piano teacher for my weekly piano lesson. In order to save my parents a trip into town to get me, Grandma would pick me up after my piano lesson and take me to her house where I would spend the night.

Those Thursday nights became very special to me. There are many things I remember about those overnights, one of which was Grandma's prayer before we ate supper. She didn't just say a quick prayer to give thanks for the food. She also prayed for a husband and wife who lived across the road from her. This young couple were not Christians. Grandma's heart was burdened for their souls. I remember sitting at that table listening to her pour out her heart to God for that husband and wife to be saved. Many times her prayers for them would cause her to weep quietly. Those prayers for the salvation of her neighbors made a lasting impression on me as a teenager.

My other family member who could not bear to let unbelievers go out into eternity without Christ was my Dad, Gene Miller. He often talked about having various unbelievers on his heart. Dad would pray for them and talk to them, pleading for them to accept Christ as their Savior.

I remember two men in particular who were brothers and lived near each other and near the little church we attended. Dad "carried a burden," as he called it, for these men for years. He would go to their homes and visit them, always during our spring and fall revival meetings, but at other times during the year as well. He not only invited them to church, but also explained the plan of salvation to them and warned them of the eternal judgment to come if they did not accept Christ. Although these men did not heed Dad's warnings, they liked him and always welcomed him into their homes. And in spite of their constant rejection of Christ and their refusal to attend church, Dad kept going back.

The wife my grandma prayed for did become a Christian after Grandma died. However, as far as I know, her husband and the two men my Dad was so concerned about all went out into eternity without Jesus as their Savior.

The Bible has these instructions for us concerning unbelievers:

- We are to pray for them (Rom. 10:1).
- We are to warn them and share the gospel with them (Mark 16:15; Rom. 10:15).
- We are not to give up because of rejection (1 Thess. 2:2).
- We are to accept the fact that not all will believe (Rom. 10:16). We are not responsible for the results of our efforts. We are responsible to pray and proclaim, leaving the results to God.

Oh, that I would more closely follow the example of Dad and Grandma in saying by my actions, "No, I cannot bear to let unbelievers go to their death without my prayers and warnings" (Prov. 24:11).

-30-

From God's Word, the Bible...

And we know that all things work together for good to those who love God, to those who are the called according to His purpose.

Romans 8:28

A Death That Led to Life

(A Reading from Tim)

It was a Saturday morning. My phone rang as I sat with my family in a donut shop. I saw that the caller was Union's Dean of Students. I knew this wouldn't be good. The Dean of Students doesn't call me on a Saturday morning with tidings of comfort and joy.

"We had a student killed in a car accident last night," he said.

I didn't know the student. I had never met her. But I will be eternally grateful for her and the impact she has had on my family.

The Union University community is a tightknit group, and the death of this student was a powerful blow for the students. I hated to see them hurt. I grieved for the family and friends of the young woman.

The following Tuesday, I went to the visitation in Nashville and was struck by how tragic and senseless it all seemed. Here was a twenty-year-old girl with a bright future. What looked like a completely random accident had changed all that, leaving heartache in its wake.

I returned home the next day. As we finished dinner on that Wednesday evening, the Scripture for our family devotion time was about the crucifixion of Jesus. I used the occasion to speak to my three children about the gospel, and I used the student's death as an example of why this was such an urgent matter.

I'm sure as the student went to her classes on Friday and prepared to travel home for the weekend, she had no idea she was so close to eternity. From every indication, she was a believer in the Lord Jesus Christ, and I'm immensely grateful for that. But if she was like most of us, she wasn't giving death a single thought on that day.

I told my children that they should consider this. I told them that they could be only an unexpected car accident away from the beginning of eternity and standing before a holy God in their sins: no advocate; no mediator; the wrath of God amassed against them.

But I also told them that there is hope. Because of what the Lord Jesus accomplished through His sinless life, His sacrificial death, and His triumphant resurrection, they didn't need to fear meeting God. All they had to do was trust in Christ and His work on their behalf—to believe in the gospel—and they would be saved.

My ten-year-old son, Daniel, was especially moved as he sat and listened. Later that night, after I put the kids to bed, Daniel came out of his room with tears in his eyes, saying he wanted to be a Christian.

I talked with him about what that means, and I truly believe my precious son was converted that night. This was God's answer to the prayers we have offered for his salvation for years. Daniel later said that it was the student's death that got him to thinking seriously about the state of his soul.

The young woman's death was a terrible tragedy, and I know the lives of her loved ones will never be the same. We don't understand why God allows such things to happen, and we may never know. But we do know that God is good, that He cares for His people, and that He will work all things together for the glory of His name and the good of His people.

I do not give thanks for the tragic accident that took the life of this precious young lady. I consider it to be the fruit of the sin and rebellion that have so thoroughly ravaged God's perfect creation. I hated getting that phone call. I hated the pain and the grief the accident caused. I hate it still.

I do, however, thank God with all my heart that He is a master designer and weaver. He took the tragedy of this death and used it for something glorious and good—the salvation of my son.

The impact of this student's life didn't stop with her death, and God in His providence has forever intertwined her with my family. Though I never met her in this life, I look forward to doing so in the life to come.

-31-

From God's Word, the Bible...

He who sits in the heavens shall laugh;
The Lord shall hold them in derision.
Then He shall speak to them in His wrath,
And distress them in His deep displeasure:
"Yet I have set My King
On My holy hill of Zion."

Psalm 2:4-6

A Throne Set in Heaven

(A Reading from Roger)

I am troubled by the increasing anti-Christian sentiment that I am seeing. Hatred of Christianity seems to be growing by leaps and bounds. Ironically enough, much of it is coming from people who pride themselves on being champions of tolerance and equality.

Where can Christians find comfort and consolation in these trying and sinister times? Sometimes there is a ton of comfort in a mere ounce of words. So it is with Revelation 4:2. The Apostle John says: "Immediately I was in the Spirit; and behold, a throne set in heaven, and One sat on the throne."

When we come to the Book of Revelation, it is crucial for us to remember that it was originally given to Christians in seven churches. Those churches are identified and addressed in chapters two and three.

These people were in serious trouble. They were hated

for merely being Christians. Their beliefs were not politically correct. The hatred had even led to some Christians being put to death.

Those early believers might have had moments when they wondered if there is a throne—a governing authority—anywhere in this universe or if all is a meaningless, hopeless jumble. Some might have even had moments in which they thought the governing authority of this universe is set in hell.

It must have been very reassuring for them to read John's words: "... behold, a throne set in heaven.... "

The world is not just a bundle of chaos and confusion. There is a throne, and it is in heaven. Hell does not rule. Heaven does.

If heaven is ruling, why is there so much evil in this world? This will stretch your mind to the breaking point—even the evil of this world is part of the plan! We have a tendency to take evil to mean that God has vacated the throne, but He hasn't.

No, I am not saying God is responsible for the evil in this world—not for a minute! I am saying that God in His sovereign greatness and infinite wisdom is not defeated by evil but rather uses it to bring about His purposes. Does the evil cause us to be uncomfortable? Yes, but God's primary purpose is not to make us comfortable.

In these tumultuous and threatening days, we do well to frequently remind ourselves of the story of Joseph. Was it evil for him to be hated by his brothers? Definitely. Was it evil for them to sell him into slavery? Obviously. Was it evil for him to be falsely accused by Potiphar's wife and imprisoned by Potiphar? Yes. But God had a purpose in it all (Gen. 50:20).

Then there's Daniel. Ripped away from his home in Jerusalem and transported five hundred miles to Babylon! Were those evil circumstances? They most certainly were! But God was in those circumstances and used them in a glorious way. And Daniel did not let the evil of Babylon cause him to think that God was not in control but clung to the conviction that there is a God in heaven (Dan. 2:28).

There is consolation in knowing that there is a throne in heaven. There is also consolation in that word "set." The throne John saw was set in heaven. It is not only there, but it is also not going anywhere. Men can hate it and rage against it, but they cannot destroy it. The plans of earth against heaven cannot succeed, and the plans of heaven for earth cannot fail.

Is it okay to desire peace in this chaotic world? Yes, it is. But of far greater importance is being at peace with the One who sits on the throne. How can we be at peace with God? The Book of Revelation has a lot to say about the Lamb of God. That refers, of course, to Jesus. The lamb was an animal used for sacrifice. Jesus came to this earth so He could go to the cross and there be the sacrifice for our sins. The way to be at peace with the throne of God is by faith in the Lamb of God. May God help us to join in the great chorus of Revelation 5:13:

> *Blessing and honor and glory and power*
> *Be to Him who sits on the throne,*
> *And to the Lamb, forever and ever!*

About the Authors

Roger Ellsworth is a retired pastor, active in ministry and writing, who lives in Jackson, Tennessee. He and his wife, Sylvia, love the message of the Bible, and they enjoy sharing the wonderful counsel of the Word of God in language that ordinary people can understand and appreciate.

Roger has written numerous books on the Christian faith, and has exercised a preaching ministry for over fifty years. His sermons are available to listen for free on SermonAudio.com.

Tim is Associate Vice President for University Communications, Union University, Jackson, Tennessee.

Martyn is Pastor, Emmaus Road Baptist Church, Ewing, Illinois.

Other Books

Enjoy collecting the My Coffee Cup Meditations Series.

The "Thumbs-Up" Man ISBN 978-0-9988812-5-6
A Dog and A Clock ISBN 978-0-9988812-9-4
When God Blocks Our Path ISBN 978-0-9988812-4-9

www.mycoffeecupmeditations.com

www.ingramcontent.com/pod-product-compliance
Lightning Source LLC
Chambersburg PA
CBHW070623300426
44113CB00010B/1639